RESEARCH ARTICLES
IN
EDUCATION

RESEARCH ARTICLES IN EDUCATION

An Opportunity for Critical Analysis of Practical Educational Research

Robert F. Mooney, Ph.D.
Professor of Education
Salem State College
Salem, Massachusetts

Robert J. Armstrong, Ed.D.
Professor of Education
Salem State College
Salem, Massachusetts

KENDALL/HUNT PUBLISHING COMPANY
DUBUQUE, IOWA

Copyright © 1971 by Robert F. Mooney and Robert J. Armstrong

Library of Congress Catalog Card Number: 77-167933

ISBN 0-8403-0484-6

All rights reserved. No part of this publication may be reproduced, stored in a retrieval system, or transmitted, in any form or by any means, electronic, mechanical, photocopying, recording, or otherwise, without the prior written permission of the copyright owners.

Printed in the United States of America

Contents

SECTION I
MARKING AND GRADING STUDIES

1. Conventional and Non-Conventional Marking and Evaluation
   Practices in Higher Education 3
   Robert F. Mooney and *Robert J. Armstrong, Salem State College*

2. A Comparison of the Student Teaching Profiles of Present Student
   Teachers with the Current Teaching Profiles of 1969 Graduates 17
   Robert F. Mooney, Salem State College

3. A Comparison of the Types of Evaluation Systems Used
   in Student Teaching 27
   Robert J. Armstrong, Salem State College

4. Does the Quality Point Grading System Motivate Secondary School
   Students to Select Courses Compatible with Their Abilities? 36
   Warren J. Bowen, Tewksbury Public Schools

5. The Quality Point Report Card: Its Influence on Students
   and Parents 43
   Alice Marcotte and *Francis Treanor, Tewksbury Public Schools*

SECTION II
VALIDITY AND PREDICTION STUDIES

6. A Comparison of Three Methods of Placing College Freshmen in
   Advanced English Composition Courses 55
   Thomas G. Maher and *Robert F. Mooney, Salem State College*

CONTENTS

7. The NLNPNG as a Predictor of Successful Completion of the Thee Year Diploma Program at Lawrence General Hospital School of Nursing ... 61
   Marie Patricia Sheehan, School of Nursing, Lawrence General Hospital

8. Cross Validation of a Method for Selecting Children Requiring Special Services in Reading ... 65
   Harry L. Crowley, Fitchburg State College and *Bessie Ellis, Leominster Public Schools*

9. Determining the Validity and Reliability of an Attitudinal Instrument ... 74
   Michael J. Savage, Salem State College

10. Can Scores Obtained from the Slosson Intelligence Test Be Used with as Much Confidence as Scores Obtained from the Stanford-Binet Intelligence Scale? ... 81
    Robert J. Armstrong, Salem State College and *John A. Jensen, Boston College*

11. The Slosson Intelligence Test: Implications for Reading Specialists ... 86
    Robert J. Armstrong and *Robert F. Mooney, Salem State College*

12. The Influence of Test Title on Test Response ... 92
    John A. Jensen and *John A. Schmitt, Boston College*

SECTION III
CURRICULUM AND INSTRUCTION STUDIES

13. The Use of Hierarchies in the Analysis and Planning of Algebra Instruction ... 101
    Peter W. Airasian, Boston College

14. A Relationship Between Television Watching and Academic Achievement in English ... 107
    Priscilla Wetmore, Dracut Public Schools

15. The Effects of Alternations Between Conditions of Quiet and Music Upon Reading Speed and Comprehension ... 114
    Bernard M. Reardon, Peabody Public Schools

16. A Comparison of a Transformational Linguistics Program with a More Traditional Linguistics Program in Grades Five and Six ... 124
    Richard Brownell and *John P. McMath, Danvers Public Schools*

SECTION IV
ATTITUDES, VALUES AND INTEREST STUDIES

17. The Use of the Videorecorder for Changing the Self Concepts of Teachers 133
    Gary G. Baker, Hamilton-Wenham Public Schools

18. High School English and Social Science Curricula of One Semester Elective Courses: Do Students and Teachers Think They Are Better Than the Traditional Curricula of Full Year Non-Elective Courses? . . . 140
    John C. Havice, North Reading High School

19. A Comparison of Reading Preference of Second Grade Students and Parent's Selection of Children's Literature 151
    David W. Hilton, Worcester State College and
    Judith A. Shepard, Mary D. Stone Elementary School

20. A Study of Traditional and Emergent Values of Eighth Grade Students in Three Academic Groups 155
    David H. Quist and *David W. Hilton, Worcester State College*

21. The Value of Kuder Interest Profiles of Trade School Boys for Counseling 160
    Mary H. Shann, Boston University

SECTION V
CONVERGENT AND DIVERGENT THINKING

22. The Development of Logical Thinking in Children 171
    Thomas C. O'Brien and *Bernard J. Shapiro, Boston University*

23. Teaching Critical Thinking in Elementary Social Studies 181
    Francis P. Hunkins, University of Washington and
    Phyllis Shapiro, John Carroll University

24. Teachers' Ratings of Pupil Creativity 187
    Donald J. Treffinger, Purdue University and
    Richard E. Ripple, Cornell University

25. Divergent Thinking Declines in the Fourth and Seventh Grades 194
    Lisano R. Orlandi, Lowell State College

Preface

As professors of educational research we have always felt the need for a book of basic educational research readings to supplement a research methods textbook in our elementary research methods courses in education. Critical analysis of current educational studies plays an indispensable role in the development of a foundation in research methodology in education. The aim then of this book is to provide the students of such a basic course with a series of relatively simple research studies to serve as a source of classroom discussion.

Since most textbooks written for courses in research methods in education do not include such articles, students can not conveniently analyze practical applications of the research techniques they are learning. The articles in this book will allow the instructor to incorporate in his course such a practical phase.

This book contains 25 research articles, most of which represent educational research which has been conducted since 1968. Much of the research reported in this book was conducted by graduate students during their first course in research. This is of particular importance since it lends an air of realism to those students who may have the notion that one must have an advanced degree in research in order to make a contribution to his educational institution.

To complement the works of these students the book includes several investigations which represent the findings of experienced researchers. In general, one can differentiate between the student and the professional researcher by noting the school affiliation of the authors. Those research articles written by personnel of the Massachusetts Public Schools represent first attempts in educational research. Authors affiliated with colleges and universities represent more experienced educational researchers.

The articles in this book typify both survey and experimental research. In most cases they are empirical in nature, that is, data have been collected and analyzed to support the research findings. The statistical techniques used in these investigations represent a cross section of the most common techniques used in basic educational research. Reporting percentages and testing hypotheses by both non parametric and parametric methods are adequately covered. The following basic statistical tests of significance normally taught in an introductory course are included; chi square, t tests, analysis of variance, and analysis of covariance. Also, Pearson product moment correlation coefficients, rank order correlation coefficients and planned comparisions are represented in the 25 articles.

Another criterion for the selection of each article was the possibility of each article to be critically analyzed. The editors specifically looked for articles in which the authors; (1) were restricted in establishing ideal designs, or (2) could be open to student criticism in his analysis and/or interpretation of the data. Consequently, it is hoped that during the practical application phase of his course, the instructor will encourage his students to; (1) seek out the internal and external validity flaws in the studies, and (2) suggest alternate designs and statistical techniques for testing the formulated hypotheses.

In selecting the articles the editors were specifically interested in making them relevant to research methods students in the Massachusetts colleges. Consequently a majority of the research represents work done in the public schools and colleges in Massachusetts. However, because of the practicality of varied research designs and contents of the articles, instructors in institutions outside of Massachusetts should find this a useful supplement to their course work.

The articles have been arranged so that research concerning similar content areas are grouped together. At the end of each article a series of discussion questions are presented to initiate student discussions. Instructors and students are urged to augment these questions with questions of their own.

The editors wish to express their appreciation to the authors and to the journals for their permission to print or reprint the articles in this book.

Robert F. Mooney
Robert J. Armstrong

SECTION I

MARKING AND GRADING STUDIES

1

CONVENTIONAL AND NON-CONVENTIONAL MARKING AND EVALUATION PRACTICES IN HIGHER EDUCATION

ROBERT F. MOONEY and ROBERT J. ARMSTRONG
Salem State College
Salem, Massachusetts

INTRODUCTION

For purposes of this study *conventional marking system* is defined as one which has typified our schools through the past century. It is a system which uses any or all of the following: straight letter grades such as A, B, C; letter grades with signs such as A, B+, C-; numerical grades such as 94, 81, 62. A *non-conventional marking system* is one which deviates radically from the previously mentioned conventional marking system. Most non-conventional marking systems fall under or are derivatives of the following: Pass-Fail; Honors-Pass-Fail; Satisfactory-Not Satisfactory.

PURPOSE

The purpose of this study was to determine the nature of current marking and grading policies in institutions throughout the country. More specifically, this study was an attempt to determine:
1. the types of conventional and non-conventional grading systems currently being used;
2. the relative use of conventional grading systems to non-conventional systems;
3. the following aspects about non-conventional systems currently being used;
    A. whether the system is mandatory or optional,
    B. its class availability (e.g. freshman),
    C. its campus availability (e.g. selected departments),
    D. its course availability (e.g. electives only),
    E. number of courses that can be taken (e.g. per semester),
    F. whether it is converted for use in determining grade point averages,
    G. willingness to accept non-conventional transfer credit from

other institutions,
4. the degree of satisfaction of each institution with its present system.

METHOD

In attempting to gather the necessary information to conduct this investigation, the researcher constructed a 27 item questionnaire. Each of the 27 questions consisted of two parts. The first part of each item asked the participant to indicate his institution's current policy, while the second part requested him to state his degree of satisfaction with this existing policy. The instrument was pretested on seven academic deans as well as four college professors with expertise in the field of measurement and evaluation. Appropriate revisions were made to increase the instruments's validity.

The actual study sample consisted of 450 randomly selected four year accredited institutions at the national level. The contact person at each institution was the academic dean. Completed questionnaires were received from 315 of the 450 institutions (70%) asked to participate in the study. Responses were made by institutions from 47 states as well as Washington D.C. and Puerto Rico.

RESULTS

Table 1-1, Part A, is used to illustrate the number and percentage of institutions that either use conventional and non-conventional systems exclusively or use a combination of both systems. This section of the table reveals that:
1. about one third (35.23%) of the colleges reported using a conventional marking system exclusively;
2. only 1.27% of the colleges reported using a non-conventional marking system exclusively;
3. approximately two thirds (63.50%) of the colleges reported using both conventional and non-conventional marking systems to some degree.

Part B of Table 1-1 is concerned with the number and percentage of institutions using these two systems to some degree (exclusively and combined). Only four or 1.27% (Part A) of the institutions use non-conventional exclusively, thus 311 or 98.73% use conventional marking to some degree. Since 111 or 35.23% (Part A) use conventional marking exclusively, 204 or 63.77% of the institutions use a non-conventional marking system to some degree.

TABLE 1-1

Current Availability of Conventional and
Non-Conventional Marking Systems

Part A

Exclusive **or** Combined Use

Marking System	N	%
All Conventional	111	35.23
All Non-Conventional	4	1.27
Combination of Conventional and Non-Conventional	200	63.50
Total	315	100.00

Part B

Exclusive **and** Combined Use

Marking System	N	Sample N (315) % of
Some Degree of Conventional (315 − 4 = 311)	311	98.73
Some Degree of Non-Conventional (315 − 111 = 204)	204	64.77

Table 1-2 reveals the types of conventional systems currently being used, as reported by the academic deans of institutions using a conventional system to some degree. The table shows an obvious preference for letter grades, with straight letter grades a 2.5 to 1 choice over letter grades with plus and minus designations. Numerical grades are just about extinct. What is interesting to note in Table 1-2 is that 32.8% of the respondents are *not* satisfied with their present system. This seems to suggest that although 99% of the colleges use conventional marking to some degree, almost one-third of the academic deans do not seem to be satisfied with it. Many of the dissatisfied deans expressed a desire to either implement a non-conventional system or to expand their current one. A small minority of the dissenting deans indicated they wanted to change but within the framework of a conventional system. Since academic deans tend to be less responsive to change than faculty or students, this figure seems to indicate a future trend toward a change from traditional to non-conventional grading.

TABLE 1-2

Question: What type(s) of conventional marking system do you currently use?

Response	Number
Straight letter grades	216
Letter grades with plus and minus designations	86
Numerical (e.g., 80, 81, etc.)	5
Point scale system (1.0, 2.0, etc.)	66
Total	373

Note: More than one answer could have been circled; hence the unusual total.
Note: 67.22% indicated that they were satisfied with this system.

Table 1-3 reflects the responses of the academic deans, of institutions using a non-conventional system to some degree, to the question, "What type(s) of non-conventional marking system do you use?" The table clearly illustrates that "Pass-Fail" is the most popular of the non-conventional systems. Others such as Honors-Pass-Fail, Satisfactory-Not Satisfactory and High Pass-Pass-Fail were scattered responses. Note that approximately 21% are not satisfied with their policy. From their comments following the question, this dissatisfaction fell into four categories:

1. those desiring a different type of non-conventional system;
2. those desiring to expand their non-conventional system;
3. those desiring to reduce the availability of their non-conventional system;
4. those desiring to go back to a conventional system exclusively.

The majority of those dissatisfied were in the first and second category. For example, most of those in the first category indicated a desire to change from a two category system (e.g. Pass-Fail) to a three category system (e.g. Honors-Pass-Fail). Thus, although 21% dissatisfaction is reported, only a small minority of these dissatisfied deans prefer a conventional system to a non-conventional one.

TABLE 1-3

Question: What type of "non-conventional" system do you use?

Response	Number	Percent of Total
Pass-Fail	145	71.08
Honors-Pass-Fail	17	8.34
Other	42	20.58
Total	204	100.00

Note: 78.97% of the respondents are satisfied with this policy.

The remaining tables (1-4—1-13) deal exclusively with non-conventional systems. They reveal the responses of the academic deans of those institutions which use a non-conventional system to some degree.

TABLE 1-4

Question: When a non-conventional ssytem is used, what percentage of your courses use this evaluation system?

Percent of Courses Evaluated Non-Conventionally	N	Percent of Total	Percent of Colleges Using More Non-Conventional
1	49	27.37	72.63
2	19	10.61	62.02
3	8	4.46	57.56
4	2	1.11	56.45
5	28	15.64	40.81
6-10	25	13.96	26.85
11-25	24	13.40	13.45
26-50	4	2.23	11.22
51-75	2	1.11	10.11
76-90	4	2.23	7.88
91-99	10	5.66	2.23
100	4	2.23	0.00
Total	179	100.00	

Note: Twenty-five colleges did not respond to this question, thus, the N reported in this table is only 179 (204—179 = 25).

8 | MARKING AND GRADING STUDIES

Approximately two-thirds (Table 1-1) of the institutions use non-conventional evaluation to some degree. However, Table 1-4 reveals that, when it is used, its use is limited for the most part. For example, 27.37% of the colleges indicated that it is used in only one percent of their courses, or stated another way 72.63% use it in more than one percent of their courses. This limited or restricted use is further illustrated by the following:
1. 40% use it in more than 5% of their courses;
2. 26% use it in more than 25% of their courses;
3. 26% use it in more than 50% of their courses;
4. 8% use it in more than 90% of their courses.

Only four institutions or 2.23% of the institutions using a non-conventional system, use non-conventional marking exclusively.

Table 1-5 reveals that, in those courses in which non-conventional marking is available, about 52% of the colleges insist on a non-conventional mark only, whereas, approximately 46% allow the student his choice. A fairly large 16.2% of the responding deans were not satisfied with their policy. The written comments of these deans indicated that they felt that once a policy has been adopted, all students should adhere to it. In other words, these deans were suggesting that once a course has been established as a non-conventional course, this should be the only system open to the student.

TABLE 1-5

Question: Is your present Non-Conventional Marking System mandatory for students?

Response	Number	Percent of Total
No	93	45.59
Yes	107	52.45
No Response	4	1.96
Total	204	100.00

Note: 83.85% of the respondents are satisfied with this policy.

Table 1-6 clearly indicates the popularity of non-conventional grading in the upper classes. The majority of the 13.3% of the deans that were not satisfied commented that all classes should have the same opportunity for this type of grading. A few deans, however, wanted to exclude the system from freshmen.

Most of the dissenting deans commented that selected schools or departments should not be the only ones using non-conventional marking. However, it is obvious from Table 1-7, that in general, when the system is applied, it is applied uniformly throughout the university. It is the researchers' opinion that, the 26.88% of the colleges in which only specific schools or departments are using non-conventional grading, fall into two major categories: (1) the system was recently started on a trial basis with one school or department as the experimenter; or (2) student teaching in the education department (or school of education) was on a Pass-Fail basis. This latter opinion is based on a recent study by the researchers which indicated that many colleges use a non-conventional marking system only in student teaching.

TABLE 1-6

Class Availability of the Non-Conventional Grading System

Class	Availability (%)
Freshman	55.73
Sophomore	70.31
Junior	85.42
Senior	88.48

Note: 86.70% of these colleges are satisfied with their policies.

TABLE 1-7

Campus Availability of the Non-Conventional Grading System

Campus Availability	% of Institutions
All Schools in University	72.58
Selected Schools in University	11.29
Selected Departments in University	15.59
No Response	0.54

Note: 88.59% are satisfied with the availability.

10 | MARKING AND GRADING STUDIES

Table 1-8 indicates that of the colleges in which non-conventional marking is available, about 15% restrict non-conventional marking to elective courses outside the student's major. Only about 14% of the colleges do not limit or restrict the availability of non-conventional marking. Of the approximately 40% who indicated "other," many commented that the system was: (1) available in student teaching only; (2) available in senior electives only; and (3) mandatory in certain courses such as physical education.

TABLE 1-8
Courses in which Non-Conventional Grading System is Available

Courses	% of Institutions
In any course	14.21
Only in elective course outside the student's major	43.36
Other	40.44

Note: 81.56% of the respondents are satisfied with this policy.

In Table 1-9 it becomes obvious that although two-thirds of the colleges have a non-conventional marking system available, this availability is quite limited within each college. (Note that only 50% of the deans responded to this question.) In fact, the table reveals that approximately:

1. 77% limit the student to one course per semester, with only 10% allowing the student three or more courses;
2. 69% restrict the student to three or less courses per academic year;
3. 74% limit a student to nine or less such courses throughout his four years of college.

Most of the dissatisfied deans expressed a desire to expand the number of courses a student could take under a non-conventional marking system. On the other hand, a small number of deans, mostly from institutions allowing almost exclusive non-conventional marking, stated that they wanted to reduce the availability of non-conventional courses.

TABLE 1-9

Number of Courses a Student May Take in Which a Non-Conventional Marking System Is Used: Per Semester, Per Year, Per Four Year Program

Number of Courses in One Semester	Number of Colleges Responding	Percent of Total
1	88	77.20
2	14	12.28
3	3	2.63
4	3	2.63
5 or more	6	5.26
Total	114	100.00

Number of Courses in One Academic Year	Number of Colleges Responding	Percent of Total
1	9	12.68
2	30	42.25
3	10	14.08
4	8	11.27
5	1	1.41
6	4	5.63
7	1	1.41
8 or more	8	11.27
Total	71	100.00

Number of Courses During Student's Four Year Program	Number of Colleges Responding	Percent of Total
1	7	6.60
2	3	2.83
3	2	1.89
4	23	21.70
5	10	9.43
6	21	19.86
7	1	0.94
8	10	9.43
9	1	0.94
10-19	11	10.35
20-29	4	3.77
30-39	8	7.55
40 or more	5	4.71
Total	106	100.00

Note: 78.21% of the respondents are satisfied with their college's policy regarding the number of non-conventional grading.

Table 1-10 reports that less than 10% of the colleges attempt to convert a non-conventional grade in order to weight that grade in a student's cumulative average. Most of the deans of these colleges further commented that their non-conventional system converted such terms as Honors, High Pass, etc. to designated quality points. The most typical example cited by the deans was: Honors = 4, High Pass = 3, Pass = 2, Fail = 0. Of course when a conversion scale of any type is used, the system cannot be called non-conventional in the true sense of the word. Most of the dissatisfaction was expressed by deans who wanted to drop their conversion practice.

TABLE 1-10

Question: Is there any way or means by which you convert Pass-Fail, etc. into an equivalency for use in determining the quality point average of students?

Response	Number	Percent of Total
No	171	83.82
Yes	20	9.80
No Response	13	6.38
Total	191	100.00

Note: 89.95% of the respondents are satisfied with the "convert" or "not-convert" policy of their college.

From Table 1-11 it can be seen that less than four percent of the colleges will not accept any non-conventional transfer grades. Approximately 58% indicated they would accept all non-conventional transfer grades, and an additional 16% will accept all except those within the student's major. Responses under the category "other" were spread over the following, or combinations of them.
1. Will accept non-conventional transfer grades in all non major subject grades and electives within the major.
2. Will accept them only in courses in which we also use non-conventional evaluation.
3. Will accept them in any course, but a restriction is placed on the total number that can be accepted.
4. Each student is evaluated separately, acceptance of transfer non-conventional grades is dependent on his cumulative average in courses evaluated conventionally.

MARKING AND GRADING STUDIES | 13

Note that approximately 94% of the deans indicated they are satisfied with their policy. Most of the dissenting deans were in favor of expanding their acceptance of non-conventional transfer credit.

TABLE 1-11

Question: What is your policy concerning transfer credits of courses which have been taken on a Pass-Fail or similar type marking system?

Response	Number	Percent of Total
Will not accept any	7	3.43
Will not accept any for major subject area credit	33	16.17
Will accept all	119	58.34
Other	39	19.12
No Response	6	2.94
Total	198	100.00

Note: 93.58% of the respondents are satisfied with the transfer credit policy of their college.

Table 1-12 clearly indicated that non-conventional marking is not a "fad" which colleges tried for one year and then dropped. About 58% of the colleges who have such a system, have had it at least two years.

TABLE 1-12

Question: How long has a non-conventional marking system been available to your student body?

Response	Number	Percent of Total
Just started	1	0.53
One semester	21	10.29
One Year	46	20.54
Two Years	59	28.92
More than two years	60	29.41
No Response	17	8.33
Total	187	100.00

Table 1-13, reveals that 85.3% of the colleges (responding to this question) which offer at least some non-conventionally marked courses feel it is successful. This is an impressive figure considering the fact that almost two-thirds of the colleges having a non-conventional system have had it at least two years to evaluate its merit.

TABLE 1-13

Question: In your judgment has the system met with success?

Response	Number	Percent of Total
No	24	14.72
Yes	139	85.28
Total	163	100.00

CROSS BREAK RESULTS

In order to gain further insight into present marking policies in higher education throughout the country the reseachers reconstructed the previously reported 13 tables three different ways.

First, the tables were reconstructed so that the data were shown separately for small, medium and large colleges. A small college was defined as a college with an undergraduate enrollment of less than 1200 students. A medium size college was one whose undergraduate enrollment was between 1200 and 4000. A college whose undergraduate enrollment was over 4000 was considered a large college. A series of chi square significance tests were conducted and the number of significant chi squares (.05 probability level) was less than the number you would expect to obtain by chance alone. Thus, the researchers were not able to demonstrate that school size effected either marking policies or policy recommendations suggested by the academic deans.

Secondly, a similar cross break was conducted using public versus private institutions as the cross break criterion. Likewise, the researchers were not able to demonstrate that marking policies and academic dean recommendations differ significantly between public and private colleges.

Thirdly, a similar cross break was conducted using co-educational versus non-coeducational institutions as the cross break criterion. Again, the researchers were not able to demonstrate that marking policies and academic dean recommendations differ significantly.

Thus, the findings reported in each of the 13 tables were replicated three additional times. However, since the number of significant chi squares (.05 probability level) were less than that expected by chance alone, reporting of cross break information was not deemed necessary.

CONCLUSIONS

The major conclusions of this research are as follows.
1. About two-thirds (65%) of the colleges in the sample have some non-conventional marking, while approximately 99% reported using a conventional system.
2. About 1% use a non-conventional marking system exclusively, while 35% use a conventional system exclusively.
3. About 6% have more than 90% of their courses graded non-conventionally.
4. About 75% of the colleges that use non-conventional marking, use this system in less than 6% of their courses.
5. The most popular conventional grading system is straight letter grades.
6. "Pass-Fail" is the most popular of the non-conventional marking systems.
7. Although 65% of the colleges use non-conventional marking to some degree, only 26% use it in more than 25% of their courses.
8. For the most part, non-conventional marking is limited—77% of the colleges limit students to one non-conventionally evaluated course per semester.
9. Non-conventional marking is about 20% more popular in upper classes (junior-senior) courses than in lower classes (freshmen-sophomore) courses.
10. Physical Education and Student-teaching are the two most popular courses for non-conventional marking.
11. When non-conventional marking is used, it appears to be applied uniformly throughout the institution.
12. Less than 10% of the colleges attempt to convert their non-conventional gradessin order to weight their grades in a student's cumulative average.
13. Academic deans, in general, are satisfied with the marking policy of their institution.

The researchers feel that the results of this study can be justifiably generalized to all American universities since; (1) the sample was relatively large and truly random, (2) all three cross breaks showed no significant differences of response. However, the reader should keep in mind that opinions and degrees of satisfaction reported are those of the academic deans and are not necessarily indicative of the opinions of the faculties or student bodies.

Questions on the Mooney and Armstrong article.
1. Why did the authors choose to ask their questions to the academic deans rather than faculties and/or students? In what way did such a choice limit the external validity of the study?
2. Was this an empirical study? Was this an experimental study? Was this a survey study?
3. Do you feel that the sampling techniques used by the authors justified the generalizability of their results? Justify.
4. Can you cite any place in the study where the authors might have applied a Poisson distribution?
5. What reported statistic(s) substantiate(s) conclusion number 5? Conclusion number 10? Conclusion number 12?

2

A COMPARISON OF THE STUDENT TEACHING PROFILES OF PRESENT STUDENT TEACHERS WITH THE CURRENT TEACHING PROFILES OF 1969 GRADUATES

ROBERT F. MOONEY
Salem State College
Salem, Massachusetts

PURPOSE

The purpose of this study was: (1) to determine the extent to which student teaching profiles of Salem State College students reflect degree of success of future graduates who enter the teaching profession; (2) to examine the rationale underlying any differences that might be found; and (3) to present to the faculty of the Department of Education, Salem State College, data which could be used for any future consideration regarding the evaluation of student teachers.

METHOD

The sample for this study was comprised of two groups. The student teaching sample consisted of all 306 students of the class of 1970 at Salem State College who performed their student teaching during the Fall of 1969. The comparison sample in the study were those 140 teachers who graduated from Salem State for whom follow-up profile sheets were returned by their principal or department chairman, during the Spring of 1970.

The survey instrument was the single page profile rating form (Appendix A) currently being used by the Department of Education as its final evaluation form for student teaching. The profile rating sheets for the student teaching group were obtained from the chairman of the Department of Education.

The director of placement was able to provide the names of school systems where 150 of the 1969 graduates are employed as first year teachers. The same rating form was then forwarded to their Superintendent of Schools. An accompanying letter explained the purpose of the study and requested his cooperation in forwarding the rating forms to the immediate supervisor of the person in question. The percentage of return was 93%.

RESULTS

Table 2-1 lists the number and per cent of Outstanding (O), Highly Satisfactory (H), Adequate (A), and Unsatisfactory Ratings (U) of both the 1969 graduate sample and the student teaching sample.

TABLE 2-1

Number and Per Cent of Outstanding (O), Highly Satisfactory (H), Adequate (A), and Unsatisfactory (U) Ratings of the 1969 Graduates by Their Principals or Department Chairman and of the Student Teacher by Their Supervisors

	O N (%)	H N (%)	A N (%)	U N (%)	Total N
School System Ratings of 1969 Graduates	540 (19.7)	1679 (61.1)	496 (18.1)	31 (1.1)	2746
Faculty Ratings of Present Student Teachers	2706 (44.0)	2757 (44.8)	673 (10.9)	17 (0.3)	6153
Total N	3246	4436	1169	48	8899

Chi Square = 508.3; Significant beyond the .00001 probability level.

The chi square of 508.3 reported in Table 2-1 indicates that such a dissimilarity of ratings between the two groups could not happen by chance more than one time in 100,000. Put another way, any resemblance between student teaching ratings by the faculty supervisors at Salem State College and the ratings by the employers of 1969 graduates currently teaching, is purely coincidental. (The appendices A, B, C, and D of this study show the raw tabular data which are summarized in Table 2-1.)

Further inspection of the data in Table 2-1 shows that 44.0% of the ratings of student teachers are OUTSTANDING whereas only 19.7% of the ratings of the teacher graduates fall into this category. This pinpoints even further the evidence that either the college is vastly overestimating the personal qualities, professional competencies, and instructional effectiveness of its student teachers or the schools are vastly underestimating them. The former is certainly the more feasible since for 44.0% of a sample to be outstanding appears to contradict what the word outstanding means even in its most liberal interpretation.

Appendix E of this study depicts the conversion table used to convert student teaching ratings into course letter grades. By inspection of this conversion table one can see that in order to secure a course grade of 4.0 at least 128 points must be accumulated. To obtain a grade of 3.5 one must accumulate 110 points. Grades less than this are frowned upon by future employers of our graduates. Consequently, in order to meet the unwritten minimum standards of the school systems interested in Salem State's graduates, it appears that the college faculty feels obligated to rate students "O" or "H" when they really don't believe it. If this be the case, perhaps a more realistic conversion table, or, no conversion table at all, would enable student teaching profiles to be more indicative of their teaching performances.

The investigator also recommends that other possible reasons for such unrealistic student teaching profiles be investigated by the faculty. A few of these are represented by the following questions:

1. Would at least 2 unscheduled visits to the Student Teacher's classroom enable the supervisor to obtain a profile on the student teacher which would be a better predictor of success in the profession?

2. Would a pass-fail grading system enable the supervisor to make more realistic use of the O-H-A-U categories on the rating sheet?

3. Would a percentage grade be more advantageous in completing a rating sheet? For example, in lieu of O-H-A-U, would the faculty consider a scale analagous to the following?

O = Top 10% of student teachers I have supervised
H = Top 65-90%
A = Top 10-65%
U = Bottom 10%

IMPLICATION

It appears to the investigator that Salem State College has a moral and professional obligation to the student teachers, their future employers, the education profession, and to itself, to report as accurately as is possible the personal qualities, professional competencies and instructional effectiveness of its future teachers. Some general suggestions have been set forth in this study which might serve as the catalyst for attaining such accuracy. The responsibility now lies in the hands of the faculty.

However, since it can be assumed that the two groups studied in this research are large samples from equivalent populations, one fact seems quite certain from the data presented in this report, namely, STUDENT TEACHING PROFILES OF SALEM STATE COLLEGE STUDENTS DO NOT REFLECT THEIR TRUE VALUE TO THE EDUCATION PROFESSION.

APPENDIX A

STUDENT TEACHING PROFILE
for
306 Members of the Class of 1970

(The number in each cell represents the number of students who received this rating from their supervisors:)

Key: O Outstanding   H Highly Satisfactory
      A Adequate   U Unsatisfactory

	O	H	A	U	Total
I. PERSONAL QUALITIES					
A. Appearance	161	112	8	0	281
B. Voice and speech characteristics	74	170	57	0	301
C. Enthusiasm and vigor	135	128	41	1	305
D. Responsiveness to suggestion	181	75	23	1	280
E. Relationship with School Personnel	183	96	8	0	287
F. Punctuality and Reliability	191	79	17	3	290
II. PROFESSIONAL COMPETENCE					
A. Mastery of subject matter	103	174	26	1	304
B. Use of English	52	205	41	1	299
C. Application of Modern Methods	102	156	34	6	298
D. Clarity of objectives	135	138	33	0	306
E. Ability to communicate ideas	130	141	34	0	305
F. Understanding of teaching and learning processes	112	153	31	0	296
III. INSTRUCTIONAL EFFECTIVENESS					
A. Skill in planning	120	126	45	2	293
B. Implementation of plans	131	126	45	1	303
C. Directing a variety of learning experiences	130	119	36	1	286
D. Effectiveness of motivation	111	146	38	0	295
E. Skillful questioning and constructive use of responses	94	144	33	0	271
F. Exhibiting originality and initiative	115	125	44	0	284
G. Promoting healthy discipline	119	129	43	0	291
H. Administration of classroom routines	164	109	15	0	288
I. Alertness to pupil needs	163	106	21	0	290
TOTAL NUMBER OF RATINGS	2706	2757	673	17	6153

APPENDIX B

STUDENT TEACHING PROFILE
for
306 Members of the Class of 1970

(The number of each cell represents the % of students receiving such rating from their supervisors:)

Key: O Outstanding   H Highly Satisfactory
      A Adequate   U Unsatisfactory

		O	H	A	U
I.	PERSONAL QUALITIES				
	A. Appearance	57.3	39.9	2.8	
	B. Voice and speech characteristics	24.6	56.5	18.9	
	C. Enthusiasm and vigor	44.3	42.0	13.4	.32
	D. Responsiveness to suggestion	64.6	26.8	8.2	.35
	E. Relationship with School Personnel	63.8	33.4	2.8	
	F. Punctuality and Reliability	65.9	27.2	5.9	1.00
II.	PROFESSIONAL COMPETENCE				
	A. Mastery of subject matter	33.8	57.2	8.6	.32
	B. Use of English	17.3	68.6	13.7	.33
	C. Application of Modern Methods	34.2	52.3	11.4	2.00
	D. Clarity of objectives	44.1	45.1	10.5	
	E. Ability to communicate ideas	42.6	46.2	11.1	
	F. Understanding of teaching and learning processes	37.8	51.7	10.5	
III.	INSTRUCTIONAL EFFECTIVENESS				
	A. Skill in planning	41.0	43.0	15.4	.68
	B. Implementation of plans	43.2	41.6	14.9	.33
	C. Directing a variety of learning experiences	45.5	41.6	12.6	.34
	D. Effectiveness of motivation	37.6	49.5	12.9	
	E. Skillful questioning and constructive use of responses	34.7	53.1	12.2	
	F. Exhibiting originality and initiative	40.5	44.0	15.5	
	G. Promoting healthy discipline	40.9	44.3	14.8	
	H. Administration of classroom routines	56.9	37.8	5.2	
	I. Alertness to pupil needs	56.2	36.6	7.2	
	TOTAL PERCENT	44.0	44.8	10.9	0.3

APPENDIX C

Follow-Up Profile of 140 1969 Graduates

(The number in each cell represents the number of teachers who received this rating from their principals or department chairmen:)

Key: O Outstanding H Highly Satisfactory
A Adequate U Unsatisfactory

	O	H	A	U	Total
I. PERSONAL QUALITIES					
A. Appearance	44	72	12		128
B. Voice and speech characteristics	16	80	32	3	131
C. Enthusiasm and vigor	46	65	19		130
D. Responsiveness to suggestion	47	68	12	2	129
E. Relationship with School Personnel	50	73	10		133
F. Punctuality and Reliability	65	56	8	2	131
II. PROFESSIONAL COMPETENCE					
A. Mastery of subject matter	19	94	17	1	131
B. Use of English	17	92	20		129
C. Application of Modern Methods	22	83	26	1	132
D. Clarity of objectives	15	96	27	2	140
E. Ability to communicate ideas	13	87	25	1	126
F. Understanding of teaching and learning processes	12	91	25	2	130
III. INSTRUCTIONAL EFFECTIVENESS					
A. Skill in planning	19	83	24	2	128
B. Implementation of plans	18	82	28	2	130
C. Directing a variety of learning experiences	17	78	34	1	130
D. Effectiveness of motivation	16	83	31	1	131
E. Skillful questioning and constructive use of responses	9	79	37	1	126
F. Exhibiting originality and initiative	16	78	32	1	127
G. Promoting healthy discipline	30	67	27	5	129
H. Administration of classroom routines	26	89	27	2	144
I. Alertness to pupil needs	23	83	23	2	131
TOTAL NUMBER OF RATINGS	540	1679	496	31	2746

APPENDIX D

Follow-Up Profile of 140 1969 Graduates

(The number in each cell represents the % of teachers receiving such rating from their principals or department chairmen:)

Key: O Outstanding   H Highly Satisfactory
      A Adequate   U Unsatisfactory

	O	H	A	U
I. PERSONAL QUALITIES				
A. Appearance	34.4	56.3	9.3	0
B. Voice and speech characteristics	12.2	61.1	24.4	2.3
C. Enthusiasm and vigor	35.4	50.0	14.6	0
D. Responsiveness to suggestion	36.4	52.7	9.3	1.6
E. Relationship with School Personnel	37.6	54.9	7.5	0
F. Punctuality and Reliability	49.6	42.7	6.1	1.5
II. PROFESSIONAL COMPETENCE				
A. Mastery of subject matter	14.5	71.8	13.0	0.7
B. Use of English	13.2	71.3	15.5	0
C. Application of Modern Methods	16.7	62.9	19.7	0.8
D. Clarity of objectives	10.7	68.6	19.3	1.4
E. Ability to communicate ideas	10.3	69.4	19.3	.8
F. Understanding of teaching and learning processes	9.2	70.0	19.2	1.5
III. INSTRUCTIONAL EFFECTIVENESS				
A. Skill in planning	14.8	64.8	18.8	1.6
B. Implementation of plans	13.8	63.1	21.5	1.5
C. Directing a variety of learning experiences	13.1	60.0	26.2	0.8
D. Effectiveness of motivation	12.2	63.1	21.5	1.5
E. Skillful questioning and constructive use of responses	7.1	62.7	29.4	0.8
F. Exhibiting originality and initiative	12.6	61.4	25.2	0.8
G. Promoting healthy discipline	23.3	51.9	20.9	3.9
H. Administration of classroom routines	18.1	61.8	18.8	1.4
I. Alertness to pupil needs	17.6	63.4	17.6	1.5
TOTAL PERCENT	19.7	61.1	18.1	1.1

MARKING AND GRADING STUDIES | 25

APPENDIX E

TABLE FOR CONVERTING RAW SCORES FROM STUDENT TEACHING PROFILE TO POINT GRADE

Dervice RAW SCORE by multiplying total number of checks in the*

O column by 4
H column by 3   and then adding all products
S column by 2
U column by 1

	POINT GRADE	RAW SCORE
	4.5	143-145
	4.4	140-142
A	4.3	137-139
	4.2	134-136
	4.1	131-133
	4.0	128-130
	3.9	125-127
	3.8	122-124
	3.7	118-121
B	3.6	114-117
	3.5	110-113
	3.4	106-109
	3.3	102-105
	3.2	98-101
	3.1	94- 97
	3.0	90- 93
	2.9	86- 89
	2.8	82- 85
C	2.7	78- 81
	2.6	74- 77
	2.5	70- 73
	2.4	66- 69
	2.3	62- 65
	2.2	58- 61
	2.1	54- 57
	2.0	51- 53
	1.9	48- 50
	1.8	45- 47
D	1.7	42- 44
	1.6	39- 41
	1.5	36- 38

*Personal Qualities X 1
Professional Competence X 2
Instructional Effection X 2

26 | MARKING AND GRADING STUDIES

Questions on the Mooney article.
1. In the RESULTS section, the author recommended several possible reasons for the unrealistic student teaching profiles. What additional areas do you think should be investigated?
2. Do you agree with the assumption made by the author that the two groups studied are from "equivalent populations?" Explain your answer.
3. Discuss the acceptability of the sampling technique. What changes, if any, would you have made?
4. Individuals in one group were evaluated as student teachers while individuals in the other group were evaluated as regular teachers. What effect, if any, do you think this had on the distribution of ratings of the two groups?

3

A COMPARISON OF THE TYPES OF EVALUATION SYSTEMS USED IN STUDENT TEACHING

ROBERT J. ARMSTRONG
Salem State College
Salem, Massachusetts

INTRODUCTION

One of the most controversial areas on college campuses today is that of student evaluation. A major concern in this issue is whether the traditional conventional marking system (e.g. letter grades) should be maintained, or if some type of non-conventional marking system (e.g. Pass-Fail) should be initiated. Recently, it has been suggested by many educators that student teaching would be a natural for a non-conventional evaluation system. Although the literature is sparse concerning this topic, there is evidence that some institutions currently use a non-conventional evaluation system for student teaching while others are giving it serious consideration.

PURPOSE

The purpose of this study was to determine the following aspects of evaluation systems in student teaching for state colleges and universities:
1. the types of evaluation systems currently being used;
2. the overall degree of satisfaction with existing evaluation systems;
3. whether institutions desire to keep their current evaluation systems or desire to implement change;
4. whether institutions, regardless of their own type of evaluation system, are willing to accept non-conventional credit for student teaching;
5. whether the attitudes of student teachers, college faculty, cooperating school supervisors, and cooperating school administrators, either currently using or having been evaluated under a non-conventional system, are either favorable or unfavorable;
6. whether institutions currently using a non-conventional system have had difficulty in either obtaining or retaining student teach-

ing stations;
7. whether students evaluated under a non-conventional system have experienced difficulty in obtaining their first teaching positions upon graduation;
8. whether institutions currently using a non-conventional evaluation system convert their marks or symbols for use in computing grade point averages.

METHOD

The study was conducted at the Center for Educational Research (CER) at Salem State College. Salem is one of ten state colleges in Massachusetts. Thus, in an attempt to determine the characteristics of other similar type institutions, the study sample was limited to state colleges and universities at the national level.

In attempting to gather the necessary information to conduct this investigation, the researchers constructed a questionnaire. The instrument was pretested on four Directors of Student Teaching as well as four college professors with expertise in the field of measurement and evaluation. Appropriate revisions were made to increase the instrument's validity.

The actual study sample consisted of 100 randomly selected state colleges and universities at the national level. A questionnaire concerning evaluation in student teaching was sent to the Director of Student Teaching of the participating institutions. The percentage of returns was 93 per cent. However, it should be noted that in the tables describing the results of this survey, the sample size (N) is reported as 96, not 93. The reason for this is due to the fact that three institutions use both conventional and non-conventional systems.

RESULTS

Table 3-1 compares the number of institutions currently using conventional and non-conventional evaluation for student teaching. Fifty-nine (61%) of the institutions indicated that they currently use a conventional system, while usage of a non-conventional system was reported by 37 (39%) institutions. The chi square test of significance was used to test the null hypothesis of no difference between the number of institutions currently using conventional evaluation and the number using non-conventional evaluation. The chi square value of 5.04 reported in Table 3-1 was greater than the value (3.84) necessary to reach significance at the .05 probability level. Thus, it was concluded that a significantly large number of institutions currently use a conventional system rather than a non-conventional system.

TABLE 3-1

Chi Square Test of Significance between Institutions Currently Using Conventional and Non-Conventional Marking Systems

	Observed N	%	Expected N	Chi Square
Conventional	59	(61)	48	5.04*
Non-Conventional	37	(39)	48	

*$p < .05$ (Significant at the .05 probability level)

Table 3-2 is a 2 x 2 contingency table showing, for both the conventional and non-conventional groups, their desire either to keep their present system (No Change) or change their system (Change). The table reveals that 95% of institutions currently using a non-conventional system want to keep it (No Change), while only 33% of institutions currently using a conventional system want to keep it (No Change). The chi square value of 31.8 reported in Table 3-2 indicates that the null hypothesis of no difference between the conventional and non-conventional groups concerning their desire to keep or change their present system was able to be rejected at the .001 probability level. Thus, it was concluded that:

1. institutions currently using conventional evaluation tend to be dissatisfied with it and desire to change to a non-conventional system;
2. institutions presently employing non-conventional evaluation systems tend to be satisfied and do not desire to change to a conventional system.

TABLE 3-2

Chi Square Test of Significance between the Attitudes of Institutions Using Conventional and Non-Conventional Evaluation Systems Toward Change From Their Current Evaluation System

	Conventional N	%	Non-Conventional N	%	Chi Square
No Change	20	(33)	35	(95)	31.8*
Change	39	(67)	2	(05)	

*$p < .001$ (Significant beyond the .001 probability level)

TABLE 3-3

Current Types of Marking Systems
Part A
Conventional Marking Systems

Terminology	N	%
Straight letter grade	52	(88)
Letter grades with ±	5	(8)
Numerical Scale (e.g. 80, 81)	2	(4)
Total N	59	

PART B

Non-Conventional Marking Systems

Terminology	Code	N	%
Pass—Fail	P — F	18	(49)
Pass—No Pass	P — NP	2	(5)
Credit—Fail	C — F	1	(3)
Credit—No Credit	C — NC	1	(3)
Satisfactory—Unsatisfactory	S — U	10	(27)
Honors—Pass—Unsatisfactory	H — P — U	2	(5)
Honors—Satisfactory—Unsatisfactory	H — S — U	2	(5)
Pass—Incomplete—No Record	P — I — NR	1	(3)
Total N		37	

Table 3-3 is used to illustrate the types of evaluation or marking systems currently being used. Part A is concerned with the various types of conventional systems. Three different conventional systems were reported: (1) straight letter grades; (2) letter grades with ±; and (3) a numerical scale. Of the 59 institutions reporting that they currently use a conventional system, 52 (88%) use straight letter grades, while 5 (8%) use letter grades with ±, and 2 (4%) use a numerical scale.

The various types of non-conventional systems reported by the 37 institutions currently using them are illustrated in Part B of Table 3-3. Although many different types were reported, they can be collapsed into using either two categories or three categories for evaluation. Note that 87% use a two-category system while only 13% use three categories for evaluation. Also, 77% of those using a non-conventional system employ either P-F or S-U (Pass-Fail, or Satisfactory-Unsatisfactory).

The last type listed in Table 3-3, Part B (P-I-NR) needs to be explained more fully. Under this system, a student receives "Pass" (P) if he successfully completes student teaching. If for some reason he does not complete it successfully, he receives an "Incomplete" (I). The student then has one semester to make this up. If he is successful, the I is changed to a P. If he is not successful the second time or elects not to attempt it a second time, the I is changed to "No Record" (NR). However, it should be noted that NR is not placed or recorded on the student's transcript. This means that No Record of the student's ever attempting student teaching is recorded. Thus, after one semester, only one type of grade can be part of a student's official transcript, namely, "Pass" or P.

The responses of the Directors of Student Teaching to the question, "Would you accept or reject transfer credit for a student's non-conventional mark in student teaching?", are reported in Table 3-4. The table shows that 86 (90%) of the institutions would accept it. The extremely large chi square value (60.16) reported was far beyond the value of 10.83 necessary to reach significance at the .001 probability level. Therefore, rejection of the null hypothesis of no difference between the number of observed and expected responses to the *accept-reject* categories was possible. Thus, it was concluded that institutions, regardless of their type of evaluation system, were significantly more willing to accept rather than reject non-conventional transfer credit for student teaching. Additionally, five of the 10 institutions reporting they would reject transfer credit did so for the following reasons. Two of these five indicated that conventional marking was a state regulation

TABLE 3-4

Chi Square Test of Significance between Acceptance and Rejection of Transfer Credit for a Student's Non-Conventional Mark in Student Teaching Irrespective of the Institution's Own Evaluation System

	Observed N	%	Expected N	Chi Square
Accept	86	(90)	48	60.16*
Reject	10	(10)	48	

*$p<.001$ (Significant beyond the .001 probability level)

for certification. Three of the five indicated that rejection was based on an institutional policy which requires student teaching to be completed under its supervision, thus, transfer credit of any type for student teaching is not accepted.

Table 3-5 reveals the responses to a series of questions asked the 37 Directors of Student Teaching at institutions currently employing non-conventional evaluation systems for student teaching. It should be noted that only 35 of the 37 responded. The other two institutions had just recently implemented a non-conventional system, and the directors felt it had not been in operation long enough for them to answer questions concerning its effectiveness. The Directors of Student Teaching at each institution currently using a non-conventional system were asked to indicate whether the attitudes of student teacher, college supervisors, cooperating school supervisors, and cooperating school administrators toward non-conventional evaluation were either: (1) *favorable,* or (2) *neutral or unfavorable.*

TABLE 3-5

Chi Square Test of Significance between Favorable and Neutral or Unfavorable Attitudes of Personnel either Using or Having Been Evaluated Under a Non-Conventional System

Type of Personnel	Attitudes	Observed N	%	Expected N	Chi Square
Student Teachers	Favorable	28	(80)	17.5	12.60*
	Neutral or Unfavorable	7	(20)	17.5	
College Faculty Supervisors	Favorable	31	(89)	17.5	20.82*
	Neutral or Unfavorable	4	(11)	17.5	
Cooperating School Supervisors	Favorable	30	(86)	17.5	17.86*
	Neutral or Unfavorable	5	(14)	17.5	
Cooperating School Administrators	Favorable	32	(89)	17.5	24.02*
	Neutral or Unfavorable	3	(11)	17.5	

*$p < .001$ (Significant beyond the .001 probability level)

Eighty per cent or more of the Directors indicated that the attitudes of their personnel were favorable (Student Teachers 80%; College Faculty Supervisors 89%; Cooperating School Supervisors 86%; Cooperating School Administrators 89%).

Since the value necessary for significance at the .001 probability level is 10.83 the null hypotheses of no difference between the observed and expected frequencies of *favorable,* and *neutral or unfavorable* for all four categories of personnel were able to be rejected: student teachers 12.60; college faculty supervisors 20.82; cooperating school supervisors 17.86; cooperating school administrators 24.02. In other words, the attitudes of student teachers, college faculty supervisors, cooperating school supervisors, and cooperating school administrators either using or having been evaluated under a non-conventional system were significantly more favorable toward this type of evaluation than neutral or unfavorable combined.

Several of the Directors provided additional information concerning student attitudes. For example, some reported that a small minority of the students preferred a conventional evaluation system because high grades were usually awarded, which raised their overall grade point averages. On the other hand, the major reason reported for students preferring non-conventional evaluation was that it provided a climate for a more meaningful evaluation. That is, the elimination of conventional grades reduced anxiety and tension, and broke down the barrier between the student teacher and his supervisors which created a climate conducive to meaningful, constructive evaluation.

Ten of the 12 Directors of Student Teaching reporting neutral or unfavorable attitudes of college and/or public school personnel provided explanatory comments. An expressed desire to change back to a conventional marking system was reported only once. In this case, the cooperating school supervisors indicated that they wanted the institution to go back to using a letter grade marking system with plus and minus designation. In all other situations, the emphases were placed on changing the type of non-conventional marking and/or providing additional information. The most frequently reported reasons were as follows.

1. Change from a two category system (e.g. Pass-Fail) to a three category system (e.g. Honors-Pass-Fail).
2. In addition to a mark (non-conventional), a rating scale and/or written report should be used so that the student teacher and prospective employers will be able to get a clearer picture of the student-teacher's strengths and weaknesses.

Additionally, the Directors of Student Teaching at institutions currently using non-conventional evaluation were asked the following

three questions which must be seriously considered by an institution contemplating change to a non-conventional system.
1. Has non-conventional evaluation created a problem for your institution in either obtaining or retaining student teaching stations?
2. Do students evaluated under a non-conventional system have difficulty in obtaining their first teaching positions upon graduation?
3. Do you convert your non-conventional marks or symbols into equivalencies for use in determining quality point averages?

The results to these three questions are as follows.
1. All 35 (100%) Directors reported that non-conventional evaluation has not created a problem in either obtaining or retaining student teaching stations.
2. All 35 (100%) Directors reported that students evaluated under a non-conventional system do not have any problems in obtaining their first teaching positions.
3. Thirty-six (97%) of the Directors reported that they do not convert their non-conventional student teaching marks for use in computing grade point averages. Although it was not a part of the question most of the institutions indicated that credit to be counted toward graduation is awarded for student teaching, but it is not part of the grade point average. The one institution which indicated they use a conversion scale also reported that they wanted to eliminate it. The system in question was Honors (H), Pass (P), Unsatisfactory (U), in which H equals a grade of A, P equals a grade of B, and U equals a grade of F.

CONCLUSIONS

In summary, the results of this study, based on this sample of 93 state colleges and universities, are as follows.
1. More institutions currently use a conventional evaluation system for student teaching than a non-conventional system.
2. Institutions currently using a conventional system are much more dissatisfied than satisfied with it, and many more desire to change to a non-conventional system than to keep their present conventional system.
3. Institutions currently using a non-conventional system are much more satisfied than dissatisfied with it, and most desire to keep their system rather than change to a conventional system.
4. Institutions, regardless of their type of evaluation system, are far more willing to accept than reject non-conventional transfer credit for student teaching.

5. The attitudes of student teachers, college faculty supervisors, cooperating school supervisors and cooperating school administrators, either currently using or having been evaluated under a non-conventional system, are extremely more favorable than unfavorable or neutral combined.
6. Institutions currently using a non-conventional system have not found any difficulty in either obtaining or retaining student teaching stations.
7. Students evaluated under a non-conventional evaluation system have not had any difficulty in obtaining their first teaching positions upon graduation.
8. Institutions currently using a non-conventional evaluation system do not convert their marks or symbols for use in computing grade point averages, but credit to be counted toward graduation is awarded for student teaching.

Questions on the Armstrong article.
1. Does the fact that the sample was based on state institutions only, negate useage of the findings by non-public institutions? Explain your answer.
2. What additional areas (e.g. acceptance of transfer non-conventional credit) do you feel should have been investigated?
3. The attitudes of the student teachers, cooperating teachers, cooperating administrators, and college faculty were expressed by the Director of Student Teaching rather than by the individuals themselves. What, if any, limitations do you feel this has on reported findings of this study?
4. The researcher reported a chi square value of 31.8 in Table 3-2. Determine if the value is correct by calculating the chi square yourself.
5. The overall N for the study was 93. However, the N for colleges using a non-conventional system was only 37. What limitations did the researcher put on his findings for this latter group? What restrictions do you feel should be inflicted?

4

DOES THE QUALITY POINT GRADING SYSTEM MOTIVATE SECONDARY SCHOOL STUDENTS TO SELECT COURSES COMPATIBLE WITH THEIR ABILITIES?

WARREN J. BOWEN
Tewksbury Public Schools
Tewksbury, Massachusetts

INTRODUCTION

Recently, the Tewksbury Public Schools introduced the quality-point marking system into its senior and junior high schools. Although this type of grading system is not new, it is employed in relatively few schools throughout the country.

Basically this system of reporting student grades works as follows. All academic subjects are divided into five levels of difficulty, and a given level is assigned a certain number of points for each letter grade (A, B, C, etc.) achieved. The five levels of difficulty roughly equal the placing of students in superior, above-average, average, below average, and remedial groupings. Table 4-1 shows how quality points are assigned for each level and for each letter grade. This table applies only to Tewks-

TABLE 4-1

Quality Point Values Assigned to Teacher Letter Grades

Letter Grade	Quality Points Based on Level of Difficulty				
	1	2	3	4	5
A	8	7	6	5	4
B	7	6	5	4	3
C	6	5	4	3	2
D	5	4	3	2	1
E	0	0	0	0	0

bury as other systems would have modifications to meet their own needs.

It can be seen from Table 4-1 that the worth of A's, B's, C's, and D's varies with the difficulty level of a particular class in a particular subject. For example, a "B" in a level-1 subject would be equal to an "A" in a level-2 subject or class, each being worth seven quality points. At this point it is important to mention that the subject matter must be properly geared to the abilities of the students at a particular level. For example, the material for a U.S. History, level-5, would or should concentrate on the teaching of basic skills, such as reading, writing, and outlining rather than upon the accumulation of information about our nation's history.

The advantages of this type of a reporting system are many. The most obvious and probably the most important advantage is that students located in the lower levels should experience their share of the higher grades, if the levels are properly geared to their abilities.

Another advantage of this system centers around the compilation of class rank. Class ranking, which is so important for admission to college, is based according to letter grades achieved and levels of difficulty rather than on grades alone. It is felt that this is a more fair method of ranking students.

In the past, many students selected subjects which were below their abilities in order to obtain a high grade and a higher rank in class as well as to impress parents and college admission officials. In Tewksbury, it was thought that the quality-point system might possibly reduce or eliminate this practice. This, however, was only an assumption, and the faculty at Tewksbury was not at all sure this assumption could be supported.

PURPOSE

The purpose of this study was to determine if the quality-point marking system in the junior and senior high schools motivates students to select courses which are more challenging to their abilities. Or stated another way, its purpose was to disprove the theory that even under a quality-point marking system students do not select courses that are more challenging to their abilities.

METHODOLOGY AND RESULTS

The researcher and two faculty peers constructed a five-item questionnaire designed to determine the extent to which students would be more willing to select courses commensurate with their abilities if the

38 | MARKING AND GRADING STUDIES

quality point system were in effect. This questionnaire (see Appendix) was administered to 35 students randomly selected from each of the top and lower 30% of grades nine and twelve. Thus 140 students comprised the total sample.

The researcher subjectively established that if the quality point system were to be effective in alleviating the problem of "course selection for grade only," 75% of the sample should be willing to select a course

TABLE 4-2

Results of Preference Questionnaire—Items 1-4

Part A

Upper 30%

Item #	Grade 12 G* Mark	N	(%)	Grade 12 C** Mark	N	(%)	Grade 9 G* Mark	N	(%)	Grade 9 C** Mark	N	(%)
1	A	19	(54)	B	16	(46)	A	6	(17)	B	29	(83)
2	B	21	(60)	C	14	(40)	B	8	(23)	C	27	(77)
3	C	31	(89)	D	4	(11)	C	24	(69)	D	11	(31)
4	C	31	(89)	D	4	(11)	C	14	(40)	D	21	(60)
Totals 1-4		102	(73)		38	(27)		52	(37)		88	(63)

Part B

Lower 30%

Item #	Grade 12 G* Mark	N	(%)	Grade 12 C** Mark	N	(%)	Grade 9 G* Mark	N	(%)	Grade 9 C** Mark	N	(%)
1	A	15	(43)	B	20	(57)	A	17	(49)	B	18	(51)
2	B	20	(57)	C	15	(43)	B	22	(63)	C	13	(37)
3	C	30	(86)	D	5	(14)	C	27	(77)	D	8	(23)
4	C	30	(86)	D	5	(14)	C	28	(80)	D	7	(20)
Totals 1-4		95	(68)		45	(32)		94	(67)		46	(33)

*G refers to a student preferring the higher Grade.
**C refers to a student preferring the Challenge.

MARKING AND GRADING STUDIES | 39

for its challenge rather than for its grade with the idea that the higher quality point associated with a more challenging course would count more toward class standing.

The actual percentage was determined by comparing the total number of "prefer the higher grade" responses to the total number of "prefer the challenge" responses, for items 1-4 of the questionnaire. This was also done separately by grade, for both the upper and lower groups. Table 4-2 shows the tabular results. Only the upper group in grade 9 showed some signs of selecting a course for the challenge (Upper Group, Grade 9, $C^* = 63\%$). Only one-third or less of the other three groups indicated a willingness to select a course for the challenge rather than for the grade (Upper Group, Grade 12, $C^* = 27\%$; Lower Group, Grade 12, $C^* = 32\%$; Lower Group, Grade 9, $C^* = 33\%$).

It was stated previously, that if the quality-point system were to be effective in alleviating the problem of "course selection for grade only," 75% of the sample should be willing to select a course for its challenge rather than for its grade with the idea that the higher quality point associated with a more challenging course would count more toward class standing. Tables 4-3 and 4-4 compare the number of students who stated that course selection was based on its challenge rather than a grade. The combined responses (total, items 1-4) of the upper group grades 9 and 12 students are reported in Table 4-3, and the same combined responses of the lower group students are reported in Table 4-4. The chi square test of significance was used, for both the upper and lower groups to test the null hypotheses that the distributions of "prefer grade to challenge" and "prefer challenge to grade" do not differ from the expected distributions indicated by the researcher.

TABLE 4-3

Chi Square Test of Significance between Grade Preference and Challenge Preference for Upper 30% Group

	Observed N (%)	Expected N (%)
Prefer Grade to Challenge	154 (55%)	75 (25%)
Prefer Challenge to Grade	126 (45%)	210 (75%)
Chi Square	134.4*	

*$p<.001$ (Significant beyond the .001 probability level)

40 | MARKING AND GRADING STUDIES

Table 4-3 reveals that only 126 or 45% of the combined (grades 9 and 12) upper group students prefer the challenge to the grade, whereas, it was expected that 210 or 75% of these students would prefer the challenge to the grade. Lower group students responded similarly, as only 32.5% instead of 75% indicated that they prefer the challenge to the grade. The large chi square values of 134.4 and 269.7 reported in Tables 4-3 and 4-4 respectively were far beyond the value of 10.287 necessary to reach significance at the .001 probability level. Thus, rejection of both null hypotheses was possible. Therefore, it was concluded, that students independent of their academic standing prefer a course which would yield a high mark to a course which would present an academic challenge. This preference is significantly greater than what the faculty would accept (25%) as evidence that the quality point system was eliminating the practice of students selecting courses for the "mark."

TABLE 4-4

Chi Square Test of Significance between Grade Preference and Challenge Preference for Lower 30% Group

	Observed N (%)	Expected N (%)
Prefer Grade to Challenge	189 (67.5%)	70 (25%)
Prefer Challenge to Grade	91 (32.5%)	210 (75%)
Chi Square	269.7*	

*$p < .001$ (Significant beyond the .001 probability level)

Table 4-5 reveals the responses to Item 5 of the preference questionnaire, "Do you feel that you fully understand the quality-point marking system?" Note that only 64% of all grade 9 students and only 51% of all grade 12 students indicated that they fully understood the quality point system. It is also interesting to note that a larger percentage of students in the "upper 30%" group in both grades stated that they understood the system, compared to students in the "lower 30% group."

The overall study results are somewhat tainted by the fact that only 58% of the 140 students indicated that they fully understood the quality point system. Thus, the investigation suggests, that perhaps the reason

MARKING AND GRADING STUDIES | 41

TABLE 4-5

Results of Preference Questionnaire Item 5,
"Do you feel that you fully understand the
quality-point marking system?"

	YES N (%)	NO N (%)
Grade 9		
Upper 30%	28 (80)	7 (20)
Lower 30%	17 (49)	18 (51)
Total Grade 9	45 (64)	25 (36)
Grade 12		
Upper 30%	21 (60)	14 (40)
Lower 30%	15 (43)	20 (57)
Total Grade 12	36 (51)	34 (49)
Grades 9 and 12 Combined		
Upper 30%	49 (70)	21 (30)
Lower 30%	32 (46)	38 (54)
All	81 (58)	59 (42)

that students desire to select less challenging courses in order to obtain a higher grade is that they do not realize exactly how the quality point system will neutralize the stringent grade requirement of a more demanding course. The researcher therefore suggests that the quality point system has much merit, but, in order that it be successful, the principals and department chairman of Tewksbury High School and Junior High School must thoroughly instruct all students and parents in the objectives, operation, and value of the system.

That they have not instructed students on the quality point system is especially obvious for the "lower 30%" group in grades 9 and 12, where more than 50% of the students have answered "no" to question 5 indicating that they do not understand the system.

DISCUSSION

The quality point system is so constructed that academically low students do not have to be frustrated by continually low grades and that academically bright students can be challenged without fear that an occasional low grade will hurt them. However, tangible evidence that this system will work is not present at Tewksbury. In order to give this theoretically sound system an opportunity to prove itself, this research suggests that a thorough and continual indoctrination program be instigated for all involved. Next year, a study similar to this one could determine the extent to which an indoctrination program would be able to present tangible evidence that the quality point system will motivate students to meet academic challenges.

APPENDIX

Student Questionnaire

As you now are fully aware, the quality-point marking system began in Tewksbury last September. With the understanding that A's, B's, C's etc. are now worth a different number of numerical points, depending upon the level of difficulty for the course, would you please answer the following questions as honestly as possible.

Please circle your preferred answer at the extreme right hand side of the paper.

Please answer *all* questions. Your name is not necessary.

Note: Assume for the sake of the questionnaire that your ability in school would be suitable for any of the five levels.

1. Would you prefer a grade of "A" in a level II course or a "B" in a level I course?   A   B
2. Would you prefer a grade of "B" in a level III course or a "C" in a level II course?   B   C
3. Would you prefer a grade of "C" in a level III course or a "D" in a level II course?   C   D
4. Would you prefer a grade of "C" in a level V course or a "D" in a level IV course?   C   D
5. Do you feel that you fully understand the quality-point marking system?   Yes No

Questions for the Bowen article:
1. The author states the purpose of his study is to determine if the new marking system "motivates" students to select courses which are more challenging to their abilities. Do you feel that his study actually measures "motivation"?
2. How would you justify the author's selection of 75% expected frequency?
3. What limitations does the author inflict on his findings as a result of his sampling?
4. What serious limitations do you feel exist with such a quality point system?
5. In Table 4-3, the author reports a chi square of 134.4. Determine if such a figure is accurate by calculating the chi square yourself.

5

THE QUALITY POINT REPORT CARD: ITS INFLUENCE ON STUDENTS AND PARENTS

ALICE MARCOTTE and FRANCIS TREANOR
Tewksbury Public Schools
Tewksbury, Massachusetts

Two years ago, the quality point report card was introduced in the secondary grades of the Tewksbury Public Schools. At that time students and their parents were instructed in the meaning of the quality point system with emphasis on the various academic levels of difficulty and the numerical values assigned to the marks given in each level. To determine the effectiveness of this program, a research study was undertaken at the end of the first year by Warren Bowen of the Tewksbury Schools entitled "Does the Quality Point System Motivate Secondary School Students to Select Courses Compatible with Their Abilities?" Bowen found that about 42% of the students questioned did not understand the marking system. He also found that students were concerned only with their immediate grade and were wary of selecting the more challenging course that might result in a lower mark. As a result of his study, a thorough and continued program of explanation of the marking system was offered to students in grades 7-12. Evening programs were also conducted to inform parents of the use and values of such a system. In addition to this, a detailed explanation of the new quality point system was printed on the back of the report card.

This particular reporting method was adopted in the Tewksbury Public Schools after more than a year of study by the school administration and a special faculty committee. In this marking system, all academic subjects are divided into five levels of difficulty which place the students into superior, above-average, average, below average, and remedial groups. Accordingly, each level is assigned a certain number of points for each letter grade given.

Table 5-1 shows how points are assigned for each level and for each letter grade. The curriculum for each level of difficulty must be especially geared to meet the needs and abilities of these students. The subject matter for a level 1 student must be truly challenging while that for a level 5 student must be involved with developing basic skills. It should also be noted that students are grouped by ability for each major

TABLE 5-1

Quality Point Values Assigned to
Teacher Letter Grades

Letter Grade	Quality Points Based on Level of Difficulty				
	1	2	3	4	5
A	8	7	6	5	4
B	7	6	5	4	3
C	6	5	4	3	2
D	5	4	3	2	1
E	0	0	0	0	0

subject individually. For example, one might be in a level 2 English class, a level 3 science class, and a level 1 history class.

One of the major advantages of this type report card is that students in the lower groups may now be rewarded with their share of higher grades. Also, students in higher groups need not be penalized for a "B" or "C" in a subject that is truly challenging for them. It is felt that this method is a more realistic way to determine class rank and honor rolls. Class rank is based on level of difficulty and grades earned, rather than on grade alone. Students should now feel more secure in selecting a more challenging and realistic program of studies. College bound students particularly should benefit by selecting courses that will enrich their future goals. Average or below average students may now be introduced to some of the more difficult or perhaps even more interesting subjects without fear of necessarily lowering their class average.

The follow-up study reported in this article attempted to determine if students in grades 7-12 in the Tewksbury Public Schools now have a more comprehensive understanding of the quality point system, and if they are selecting courses which are more challenging to their abilities. In addition, this study attempted to determine if the parents of these same students understood and were concerned with the quality point report card.

The study was conducted in the same manner as the original one conducted by Mr. Bowen so that the results could be compared. The same questionnaire used by Bowen (See Appendix A) was administered to 35 students selected at random from each of the top and lower 30%

of grades nine and twelve. Thus 140 students comprised the total student sample. A similar but more comprehensive questionnaire was mailed to the parents of these same children (See Appendix B). A self-addressed, stamped envelope was included with the questionnaire to encourage the parent to complete and return the form.

In the original Bowen study, it was subjectively established that if the quality point system were to be effective in alleviating the problem of "course selection for grade only," 75% of the sample should be willing to select a course for its challenge rather than for its grade, with the idea that the higher quality point associated with a more challenging course would count more toward class standing. In that study, Bowen found that students were concerned only with their immediate grades, and were wary of selecting the more challenging course that might result in a lower mark.

Tables 5-2 and 5-3 report the results of this study concerning student preference in course selection for both the upper and lower 30% of grades 9 and 12. The results of this follow-up study indicate that the students still are concerned with grades rather than challenge, as all groups fell below the stated minimum acceptance. Only grade 9 stu-

TABLE 5-2

Results of Student Preference Questionnaire (Items 1-4)
Upper 30% of Class Reported in Percentages

Item #	Grade 12 G* Mark	Grade 12 G* %	Grade 12 C** Mark	Grade 12 C** %	Grade 9 G Mark	Grade 9 G %	Grade 9 C Mark	Grade 9 C %
1	A	60.0	B	40.0	A	48.8	B	51.2
2	B	74.4	C	25.6	B	53.5	C	46.5
3	C	97.1	D	2.9	C	67.4	D	32.6
4	C	78.4	D	21.6	C	62.8	D	37.2
Totals 1-4 Present Follow-up Study		72.3		27.7		58.1		41.9
Totals 1-4 Original Bowen Study		72.9		27.1		37.1		62.9

*G refers to a student preferring the higher Grade.
**C refers to a student preferring the Challenge.

dents in both groups indicated some signs of selecting a course for the challenge and the lower mark, and this was true only where the better grades of A and B were indicated. Grade 12 students in both groups showed a definite preference for the better grade and little concern for the challenge.

TABLE 5-3

Results of Student Preference Questionnaire (Items 1-4)
Lower 30% of Class Reported in Percentages

Item #	Grade 12 G* Mark	%	C* Mark	%	Grade 9 G Mark	%	C Mark	%
1	A	54.1	B	45.9	A	35.1	B	64.9
2	B	59.5	C	40.5	B	40.5	C	59.5
3	C	83.8	D	16.2	C	70.3	D	29.7
4	C	85.7	D	14.3	C	62.2	D	37.8
Totals 1-4 Present Follow-up Study		70.5		29.5		52.0		48.0
Totals 1-4 Original Bowen Study		67.9		32.1		67.1		32.9

*G refers to a student preferring the higher Grade.
C refers to a student preferring the Challenge.

Tables 5-2 and 5-3 also compare the results of this present study with the original Bowen study. About the same percentage of students in both grade 12 groups in both studies indicated a preference for the challenge and lower mark (Upper 30%; Present C = 29.5, Bowen C = 32.1: Lower 30%; Present C = 27.7, Bowen C = 27.1). A larger percentage of grade 9 lower group students in this study indicated a preference for the challenge, compared to the Bowen study (Lower 30%; Present C = 48.0, Bowen C = 32.9). It can be shown that less than 40% of all students in both studies prefer the challenge to the grade (Present study 36.8%; Bowen study 38.7%).

Table 5-4 compares the responses of students in both studies to the question, "Do you feel that you fully understand the quality-point marking system?" Grade 12 students showed a much better understanding of the system compared to the previous year's twelfth grade class; however, the grade 9 students did not make such equivalent gains. In fact, the upper 30% of grade 9 students showed a loss and did not seem to understand the system as well as last year's ninth graders. In the original study, Bowen reported that 42% of all students did not fully understand the system, whereas 31% of the students in this study reported that they did not fully understand the system. Although a large percentage still do not understand it, gains have been made.

TABLE 5-4

Results of Preference Questionnaire Item 5, Reported in Percentages
"Do you feel that you fully understand the
quality-point marking system?"

Group(s)	Yes Present Study %	Yes Bowen Study %	NO Present Study %	NO Bowen Study %
Grade 9				
Upper 30%	80	70	20	30
Lower 30%	49	60	51	40
Total Grade 9	64	65	36	35
Grade 12				
Upper 30%	60	76	40	24
Lower 30%	43	71	57	29
Total Grade 12	51	73	49	27
Grades 9 and 12 Combined				
Upper 30%	70	73	30	27
Lower 30%	46	65	54	35
All	58	69	42	31

The results of the parents' questionnaire, reported in Tables 5-5 and 5-6, show that in general parents did not understand the marking system as well as did their children. Almost all of them are aware of the quality point report card, but only 55% feel it has been adequately explained to them. While 93% stated that they encouraged their children to choose subjects according to their level of ability, only 71% felt that this marking system was fair. It is interesting to note that almost half (48%) would prefer that the old type report card be used. When asked the same questions as their children concerning the choice of subjects according to challenge, parents seemed to be overly concerned with the grades

TABLE 5-5

Results of the Parent Attitude Questionnaire (Items 1-6) Reported in Percentages

ITEM #	% YES	% NO
1. Were you aware that last year we had adopted a quality point report card	92.5	7.5
2. If you answered question 1 yes, did you fully understand this marking system?	63.2	36.8
3. Do you feel that this marking system was adequately explained to you?	55.1	44.9
4. Do you feel that this marking system is fair to the student?	71.4	28.6
5. Have you encouraged your child to choose subjects in accordance with his level of scholastic ability?	92.8	7.2
6. Would you prefer that the old type report card be used?	47.9	52.1
TOTAL	70.2	29.8

TABLE 5-6

Results of the Parent Preference Questionnaire (Items 7-10) Reported in Percentages

Item #	G* Mark	%	C* Mark	%
7	A	50.0	B	50.0
8	B	46.8	C	53.2
9	C	69.8	D	30.2
10	C	68.9	D	31.1
Total 7-10		58.7;		41.3

*G refers to a parental preference to the high Grade;
C refers to a parental preference to the Challenge.

rather than the challenge, even though most of them indicated in Question 5 that they encouraged their children to choose subjects according to their ability level.

The results of this follow-up study are somewhat encouraging, but indicate that students and especially parents need more explanation concerning the merit of choosing more difficult subjects. They need to be made aware of the objectives and value of the system, and to realize that the grades by themselves do not determine rank in class. The level of difficulty of such courses is equally important. It should be emphasized that a somewhat lower letter grade in a more difficult level will equalize with a higher grade in a less difficult level.

Besides providing a more equitable means of determining the rank in class which colleges require, the quality point system encourages constant curriculum revision so that students will truly be taught at appropriate ability levels. It also provides a means for slower students to be rewarded for conscientious and diligent study.

If this program is to achieve these goals, a continual indoctrination program must become part of the school curriculum. This type of information is more effectively presented in small classroom discussion groups rather than in an assembly type program. Perhaps English teachers at both secondary levels could devote one class period at the beginning of the year and another immediately after the first report card to discuss the quality-point system with their students. (English was mentioned only because all students at each grade level study this subject.) A guide for teaching the system could be drawn up by the administration so that all teachers would cover the same information. If an effective program is carried out at the junior high level, then a brief review type program might be all that would be needed at the senior high level. It would be helpful it guidance counselors would discuss the point system with the students they interview.

It is more difficult to plan an educational program for parents since past attendance at this type meeting has been poor. An explanation should still be offered during the annual open house when parents are given the opportunity to follow their child's daily program, and perhaps again on the occasions when parents confer in the evening with their children's teachers. To reach parents who do not participate in evening programs, a simplified explanation of the system should be sent home with the first report card each year.

Perhaps the conclusions and recommendations reached by this research will provide the impetus for complete and successful indoctrination of the quality-point marking system to the Tewksbury Senior and Junior High School students and their parents.

APPENDIX A

Tewksbury Junior High School

Tewksbury, Massachusetts

STUDENT QUESTIONNAIRE

As you now are fully aware, the quality-point marking system began in Tewksbury a year ago last September. With the understanding that A's, B's, C's, etc. are now worth a different number of numerical points, depending upon the level of difficulty for the course, would you please answer the following questions as honestly as possible.

Please circle your preferred answer at the extreme righthand side of the paper.

Please answer *all* questions. Your name is not necessary.

Note: Assume for the sake of the questionnaire that your ability in school would be suitable for any of the five levels.

1. Would you prefer a grade of "A" in a level II course or a "B" in a level I course?   A B
2. Would you prefer a grade of "B" in a level III course or a "C" in a level II course?   B C
3. Would you prefer a grade of "C" in a level III course or a "D" in a level II course?   C D
4. Would you prefer a grade of "C" in a level V course or a "D" in a level IV course?   C D
5. Do you feel that you fully understand the quality-point marking system?   Yes No

APPENDIX B

Tewksbury Junior High School

Tewksbury, Massachusetts

PARENT'S QUESTIONNAIRE

Parents:

The quality point marking system has been in effect in Tewksbury for two school years. Depending on the level of difficulty of the particular course, A's, B's, C's, etc. are worth a different number of numerical points toward class standing. Would you please answer the following questions to aid us in determining the effectiveness of this marking system.

Please return this questionnaire in the enclosed envelope within 3 days to the Junior High School.

1. Were you aware that last year we had adopted a quality point report card?   Yes No
2. If you answered question 1 yes, did you fully understand this marking system?   Yes No
3. Do you feel that this marking system was adequately explained to you?   Yes No
4. Do you feel that this marking system is fair to the student?   Yes No
5. Have you encouraged your child to choose subjects in accordance with his level of scholastic ability?   Yes No
6. Would you prefer that the old type report card be used?   Yes No
7. Would you prefer your child to receive a grade of "A" in a level II course or a "B" in a level I course?   A B
8. Would you prefer your child to receive a grade of "B" in a level III course or a "C" in a level II course?   B C
9. Would you prefer your child to receive a grade of "C" in a level III course or a "D" in a level II course?   C D
10. Would you prefer your child to receive a grade of "C" in a level V course or a "D" in a level IV course?   C D

Questions on the Marcotte and Treanor study.
1. After reading this study and the previous one (Bowen), do you feel that the Tewksbury Public Schools are putting their new marking system to better use than they did at the time of the Bowen Research? Clarify your feelings.
2. Unlike the Bowen study, the author chose not to perform any statistical tests of significance. On the basis of the reported data in this study can you suggest any differences in student or parent answers which you would like to have tested for significance?
3. Choose a test of significance for one of your above suggestions. Perform the test and interpret your results.
4. Referring to Table 5-5, why do you think that almost 50% of the parents would prefer the old type report card?

SECTION II

VALIDITY AND PREDICTION STUDIES

6

A COMPARISON OF THREE METHODS OF PLACING COLLEGE FRESHMEN IN ADVANCED ENGLISH COMPOSITION COURSES

THOMAS G. MAHER and ROBERT F. MOONEY
Salem State College
Salem, Massachusetts

PURPOSE

Mostly every college English department chairman is familiar with the difficulties surrounding the matter of advanced placement in composition. The questions that are usually raised are of the following nature: Is the present method of placing freshmen adequate for the purposes of the department? If not, is there a better way? Can a method be devised that will accurately predict student success in composition? Perhaps, a more basic question would be; can the skills of English composition be taught at all? But this last question is surely beyond the limits of this study.

At Salem State College, the English Department, for lack of a better method, has been determining which incoming freshmen go into the advanced composition sections on the basis of an arbitrarily selected minimum College Entrance Examination Board (CEEB) English achievement score of 600. However, in light of this relatively high standard for determining placement, the department was not pleased with achievement in this course. Thus, it was also a goal of this study to determine if some other criterion might be more appropriate for assuring a greater percentage of high achievers.

Three methods of placing college freshment in Advanced Placement English Composition courses were compared in this study. The purpose of these comparisons was to determine if variables other than CEEB English achievement scores are better predictors of student success in those advanced courses.

The total number of advanced placement freshmen for the first semester classes was 114, from which a sample of 20 high and 20 low grade point average (GPA) scores in the Freshman Advanced Placement Composition course was randomly selected. In the 40 selected, the GPA results ranged from A (superior) to F (failing). Table 6-1 summarizes these selections.

TABLE 6-1

Distribution of Semester GPA (Letter Grades) for the 20 High and 20 Low Students in Freshman Advanced Placement Composition

20 High Letter Grades		20 Low Letter Grades	
N	Letter Grade	N	Letter Grade
12	A	1	C+
2	A—	10	C
6	B+	1	C—
		3	D
		5	F

An IBM print-out from the admissions office provided a fairly complete run-down of academic information about each freshman, including such data as CEEB English achievement scores, SAT verbal and math scores, rank in high school class, and converted rank in class. It was from this admissions report that most of the data for this study were gathered.

Based on the pertinence and availability of data, the investigators decided to examine individually the correlation between the students' GPA and three other factors: (1) CEEB English achievement scores, (2) SAT verbal scores, and, (3) combined CEEB and SAT V scores.

Hypotheses

Three research hypotheses were formulated for statistical testing:

$1H_1$ — There is a relationship between CEEB English achievement scores and the students' GPA.

$2H_1$ — There is a relationship between SAT verbal scores and the students' GPA.

$3H_1$ — There is a relationship between the combined scores of CEEB English achievement and SAT verbal with the students' GPA.

The three null hypotheses were:

$1H_0$ — There is no correlation between the CEEB English achievement scores and the students' GPA.

$2H_0$ — There is no correlation between the SAT verbal scores and the students' GPA.

$3H_0$ — There is no correlation between the combined scores of CEEB English achievement and SAT verbal with students' GPA.

DESIGN AND RESULTS

In order to ascertain the extent to which the CEEB English achievement scores correlated with the students' GPA, it was first necessary to assign a numerical score to the letter grades of each student. Their first semester grades were converted from letter to numerical grades in order to obtain GPA which could assume an underlying continuum. The following conversions were used: A = 4, B = 3, C = 2, D = 1, and F = 0.

These numerical grades were correlated with the coinciding CEEB scores from the admissions office.

TABLE 6-2

Correlation between CEEB English Achievement Scores and GPA of Students Enrolled in Freshman Advanced Placement Composition

	CEEB Scores	GPA
N	40	40
Mean	624.75	2.55
SD	25.5	1.36
r (Pearson-Product)		.08*

*Not significant at the .05 level.

As indicated in Table 6-2, the Pearson Product Moment correlation between GPA and CEEB English achievement was found to be .08. This did not reach significance at the .05 probability level, thus null hypothesis 1 was not able to be rejected. In other words, it appears that any relationship between CEEB English achievement scores and Advanced Placement English GPA is strictly a chance relationship, and, that these CEEB English achievement scores presently being used for placement purposes are in fact worthless in predicting academic success in the Advanced Placement Composition courses.

TABLE 6-3

Correlation between SAT Verbal Scores and GPA of Students Enrolled in Freshman Advanced Placement Composition

	SAT Verbal Scores	GPA
N	40	40
Mean	565.75	2.55
SD	37.3	1.36
r (Pearson-Product)		.17*

*Not significant at the .05 level.

The next part of the study dealt with the relationship between SAT verbal scores and students' GPA's. The statistical investigation reported in Table 6-3 shows that SAT V scores would be a slightly better method of placing students in advanced English composition classes. However, this correlation coefficient of .17 also did not reach statistical significance at the .05 probability level. Hence null hypothesis 2 was not able to be rejected, precluding any valuable use of the SAT verbal scores for placing students in the Advanced Placement Composition courses.

TABLE 6-4

Correlation of the Combined Scores on CEEB English Achievement and the SAT with Grade Point Average (GPA) of Students Enrolled in Freshman Advanced Placement Composition

	Combined CEEB SAT Scores	GPA
N	40	40
Mean	1190.25	2.55
SD	74.3	1.36
r (Pearson-Product)		.38**

**Significant beyond .05 level.

The results from the third correlation, reported in Table 6-4, were encouraging. The combined score method was shown to be a more valid way of placing freshmen in advanced composition. The correlation of .38 is statistically significant beyond the .05 probability level. Thus, we were able to reject null hypothesis 3 and conclude that such a significant correlation between the combined CEEB English-SAT V scores and Advanced Placement Composition GPA could occur by chance less than five times in 100.

Once it was established that the combined CEEB English-SAT V scores were the best of the three considered variables for predicting Advanced Placement Composition GPA for our sample, the next step was to devise a method that would predict a cut-off point for student success in Advanced Placement Composition. "Success" is loosely defined in terms of A and B grades. The underlying assumption here is that there should be mostly A and B grades with only a few "C and below" grades in an advanced placement course of this type.

Since, of the variables investigated, the combined CEEB English and SAT V scores have shown to have the highest correlation with Advanced Placement Composition GPA, a combined score necessary for a predicted minimum GPA of 3.00 (a grade of B-) was computed using the following straight line equation

$Y' = a + bX$

where: Y' = predicted score on combined CEEB English and SAT V tests necessary for a 3.00 GPA in Freshman English

$a = 1082.3$
$b = 37.9$
$X = 3.00$
therefore: $Y' = 1082.3 = 37.9(3.00)$
$Y' = 1196$

Therefore, based on this study, it would be necessary for a student to have a minimum combined CEEB English and SAT V Score of 1196 to assure achieving a B- grade.

It must be remembered, however, that although the .38 correlation coefficient between CEEB English-SAT V scores and GPA was significant, it was still relatively low, resulting in a standard error of estimate of 68.3. Strict interpretation of this would indicate that we are 68% confident that if an individual receives a GPA = 3.00, then, he had received combined CEEB-SAT V scores between 1128 and 1264. In other words, 1128 and 1264 are the 68% confidence limits within which a student must fall in order to predict a minimum B- average. Nevertheless, it remains that despite the low degree of confidence in our prediction equation, such a prediction affords the English Department with a better criterion for placing students into the Advanced Placement Composition courses.

CONCLUSION

This study has indicated that the combined CEEB English Achievement Scores and SAT verbal scores are a significantly better method than previously used, for predicting the Grade Point Average of students enrolled in the Advanced Placement English Composition courses at Salem State College.

This investigation also showed that a combined CEEB English-SAT V score of 1128 is recommended as the minimum entrance requirement to be reasonably certain that a student would maintain a B– average in an Advanced Placement English course.

It is strongly recommended that further study be done in this area in order to determine if one or more other available variables (such as rank in high school class) might be an even better predictor of academic success in Advanced Placement English. It is also suggested that a design such as this one could be used for determining criteria for other academic courses both in college and in high school.

Questions for the Maher-Mooney article:
1. What are the pitfalls in converting letter grades to numerical grades for the purpose of using more stringent statistical tests?
2. Why did the authors choose to predict college board scores from college GPA rather than the more logical predictor of GPA from college board scores?
3. What would be the 95% confidence limits of the combined CEEB-SAT V scores for predicting a B– in advanced placement English?
4. What other independent variables do you feel should be included if such a study were attempted again?
5. Outline a design which could be used for implementing a study suggested by your answer to question 4.

7

THE NLNPNG AS A PREDICTOR OF SUCCESSFUL COMPLETION OF THE THREE YEAR DIPLOMA PROGRAM AT LAWRENCE GENERAL HOSPITAL SCHOOL OF NURSING

MARIE PATRICIA SHEEHAN
School of Nursing
Lawrence General Hospital
Lawrence, Massachusetts

INTRODUCTION

Predicting the success of students desiring higher education in the various nursing programs is a monumental problem for the admissions committee of the institution to which the student applies. Many times *College Entrance Examination Board* (CEEB) scores are not available and guidance records are incomplete. Because of these factors, the National League for Nursing developed a *Pre-nursing and Guidance Examination* (NLNPNG) which is utilized in a manner similar to CEEB in college admissions.

At Lawrence General Hospital School of Nursing, Lawrence, Massachusetts, the admissions committee required students to achieve at or above the 50th percentile on the NLNPNG to be considered as a candidate. But recently, due to the success of a few "poor risk" students, the committee deleted this from the criteria for admission. Should this have been done? It was the purpose of this study to answer the question, "Is this pretest (NLNPNG) a useful predictor of success as measured by the *State Board Test Pool Examination?*" The *State Board Test Pool Examination* is a standardized test which is used in all fifty states as the sole criterion in licensing nurses.

Previous research shows several studies concerning the NLNPNG. Shaycoft (1951), a member of the National League for Nursing Research Department, correlated the NLNPNG with the *State Board Test Pool Examination* and found that the correlation coefficient was .70. She concluded that scores on the NLNPNG battery definitely are valuable aids in indicating which applicants are most likely to be successful in nursing school. Meyer (1959) conducted a similar study with similar results. This research was also supported by the National League of Nursing. Generally, it is felt in nursing that this test is of great value to admissions committees of every school of nursing in the evaluation and final selection of candidates for admission. However, the author feels that these studies are not recent and that there may be some bias involved as the same organization who writes and sells these exams also happens to evaluate the exams.

HYPOTHESIS

This research tested the null hypothesis of no significant relationship between composite scores on the NLNPNG and the *State Board Test Pool Examination*.

SAMPLE

From a total population of 81 graduate nurses, all female, of Lawrence General Hospital School of Nursing (classes of 1967, 1968, 1969), a random sample of ten graduates from each class was selected. (N = 30.)

School records of these women were reviewed in order to find the NLNPNG scores and the results of the *State Board Test Pool Examination*. As the composite score on the NLNPNG is readily available and the composite score of the State Boards is easily computed, it was decided to correlate the composite scores of each.

INSTRUMENTATION

The NLNPNG is a standardized examination prepared by the Educational Testing Service for the National League for Nursing. The exam is available to all schools of nursing for pretesting candidates. Areas of achievement tested are; reading comprehension, mathematics, natural science, and social science. Academic aptitude is also measured. Scores for each area are reported separately and a composite score can be obtained. Composite scores range roughly from 50 to 150 with an average of 100. Every candidate for admission to Lawrence General Hospital School of Nursing must take this examination.

The *State Board Test Pool Examination* is taken by the graduates of schools of nursing in order to obtain licensing. This is a standardized test which is composed of questions submitted by each of the fifty State Boards of Registration in Professional Nursing. The test is the same in each state, and recently every state accepted a score of 350 on each section as a minimum criterion for passing. Previously states had different failing points. Scoring is similar to the CEEB ranging from 200-800. A score of 350 on each of the five sections must be obtained in order to be accepted for licensing. The areas tested are: medical nursing, surgical nursing, obstetrical nursing, nursing of children and psychiatric nursing.

DESIGN AND RESULTS

The Pearson Product Moment correlation coefficient between the NLNPNG and the *State Board Test Pool Examination* was computed. The results are reported in Table 7-1.

TABLE 7-1

Correlation between NLNPNG and State Board Test Pool Examination Scores of Graduate Nurses

Exam	N	Mean	SD	r
NLNPNG	30	111	16.35	.018*
State Board	30	483.2	81.15	

*Not significant at .05 level.

The r = .018 is not significant at the .05 level of probability. The null hypothesis was therefore unable to be rejected. This means that any relationship between the scores on these exams is strictly one of chance. Thus it follows that the NLNPNG is a poor predictor of success of nursing graduates as measured by the *State Board Test Pool Examination*.

IMPLICATIONS

Instruments which predict the success of a candidate are difficult to find. This study shows that a constant review of these tools must be made in order to insure validity. Although the sample used in this study was relatively small and only represented three graduating classes, none-the-less, the results of this study strongly indicate that the NLNPNG is a very poor tool for use as a screening device at our School of Nursing. Further research must be done to find a more valid test for this purpose.

Secondly, the answer to successful prediction of nursing school achievement may lie in another type of test of high school GPA or even class rank. Thus further studies which consider such variables are suggested.

Thirdly this study did not compare scores of entrants who dropped out or who were academic failures and were not eligible to take the *State Board Test Pool Examination*. It would be interesting to look at their NLNPNG scores to see if they are substantially lower.

SUMMARY

Within the limitation of the sample used, this study has suggested to the Lawrence General Hospital that use of the *National League for Nursing Pre-nursing Guidance Examination* as a screening tool should be limited since it is a poor predictor of eventual success in nursing as measured by the *State Board Test Pool Examination*.

References

Baziak, A. Developing reliable indices to predict success on psychiatric state board examination. *Journal of Psychiatric Nursing,* March–April, 1968, 16.

Buros, O. *Tests in print.* New Jersey, Gryphon Press. The content of NLN entrance examinations. *Nursing Outlook,* February, 1963, 11, no. 2.

Meyer, B. An analysis of the results of pre-nursing and guidance achievement and state board test pool examinations. *Nursing Outlook,* September, 1959, 7.

Shaycroft, M. A validation study of the pre-nursing and guidance test battery. *The American Journal of Nursing,* March, 1951, 51.

Taylor, C., et.al. *Selection and recruitment of nurses and nursing students,* University of Utah Press, 1963.

Validation study of NLN pre-nursing and guidance examination, First Report 1961, Second Report 1962, Third Report 1963, Fourth Report 1964, Fifth Report 1965. *National League for Nursing Report.*

Questions for Sheehan article:
1. The author has suggested that further research must be done to find a more valid test for predicting success in nursing school. How would you go about finding a "more valid test"?
2. Suggest reasons why the correlation coefficient of .018 found in this study might very well be an underestimate of the relationship between the pre-nursing exam and success as a nurse.
3. If the reliability of either the predictor or criterion exam was low, how would this effect the interpretation of the author's results?
4. What steps could the author have taken to increase both the internal and external validity of her research results?
5. If you were the Dean of the Lawrence General Hospital, School of Nursing, what positive actions might you take as a result of reading this research?

8

CROSS VALIDATION OF A METHOD FOR SELECTING CHILDREN REQUIRING SPECIAL SERVICES IN READING*

HARRY L. CROWLEY
Fitchburg State College
Fitchburg, Massachusetts

and

BESSIE ELLIS
Leominster Public Schools
Leominster, Massachusetts

This study is based on the test data available for the Title I Reading Project in Leominster, Massachusetts during the school year 1969-70. The program offered special reading services through the first four grades and was concerned with assisting the purportedly disabled reader through developmental, corrective, and remedial procedures. Both public and parochial school youngsters from grades one through four in target area schools in the city were selected on the basis of the following criteria:

1. Mental ability within the normal range, although no specific IQ levels were used as cutoff points.
2. Performance on the *Metropolitan Elementary Reading Test,* Form C.
3. Inadequate classroom performance as judged by the classroom teacher and the school principal.

Reading sessions were held daily for at least forty-five minutes. Part of this time was used for enrichment activities. The special reading teachers worked with six or fewer pupils at any one time using high interest materials, both commercial and teacher-made. The program director encouraged creativity in instruction and was readily available to help each teacher in her efforts to adapt methods and materials to the individual child.

*Reprinted with permission of Harry L. Crowley and the International Reading Association.

VALIDATION TECHNIQUES

The evaluator was engaged for the program in the fall of 1969 after placement in the program already had been made and instruction had begun. Since guidelines for evaluation of Title I projects stress the evaluator's role as a technical assistant to help improve the project in progress, a check was made for reassurance that the children in the program had real reading difficulties and were not assigned solely on the basis of their need for individual attention. A technique proposed by Durost (1962), called the reading reinforced method, was applied as a cross validation of this year's method of selection with the purpose of recommending that future assignment to the program include this procedure if sufficient evidence warranted its continued use. For this article, the data from grade three only are analyzed.

The reading reinforced technique is based on the premise that a child's listening vocabulary normally will exceed his actual reading vocabulary, especially in the lower grades. Children with specific correctible difficulties will show very substantial gains in score when the teacher "reinforces" the pupil's reading by reading aloud while the child reads silently. If a child does show large gains under reinforcement, he is an excellent choice for corrective reading instruction.

All children in the classroom were given the *Metropolitan Reading Achievement Test* at their own grade level in the usual manner as directed in the Directions for Administering. A few days later, a second form of the same test was given to the class with the pupils reading the test silently while the teacher read aloud, thus "reinforcing" the child's comprehension. The second administration of the test minimized reading difficulties for the child because the test administrator's oral presentation bridged the gaps where the child's reading vocabulary alone would not suffice. Although the questions are also read orally, he still made the decision as to the correct answer himself. Comparison of the two tests determined the potential for reading improvement. If both scores were the same, the child was considered to be, in all probability, achieving at his ability level. When the reading reinforced score was substantially higher, the opportunity for improvement was considered great. The scores used were the publisher's national stanines for fall testing.

Stanines are normalized standard scores with a mean of 5 and a standard deviation of 2. Like other standard scores, stanines are comparable from test to test so long as the population on which they are based is the same. In the case of the Metropolitan series, stanines are based on an age-controlled sample at each grade level. Stanines for the Metropolitan are published for three different times during the shcool year; the fall of the year, the middle of the year and the end of the year. As stated above, fall norms were used for the original survey and for the reading reinforced testing. Spring norms were used for the follow up testing.

If the reading reinforced technique resulted in a substantial gain on the part of the student as compared to his performance under the normal conditions, this meant, according to the hypothesis of this approach, that he had a potential for improvement in his reading performance. If, at the end of the period of corrective instruction, there was also a gain in stanine position relative to the first test this meant that *more* than normal gain had taken place, presumably because of the special instruction.

The relationship between any two variables, expressed in stanines, can be shown graphically by means of the bivariate chart. The stanine bivariate approach has been used in this exploratory study to show the relationship between two sets of data; namely, the pre-test and the reading reinforced test (Figure 8-1) and the pre-test versus the post-test (Figure 8-2). Instead of plotting these bivariates in the usual way, it was possible, because of the small number of cases, to represent each case by a case number arbitrarily assigned to the children involved in this study. Each case number applies to both bivariates and only cases having complete data were used. This meant the elimination of three cases involved in the study.

The tables which follow these bivariates simply summarize in various ways the data represented in Figures 8-1 and 8-2. The interpretations of the data arrived at are those of the authors. The reader is invited to study these two figures for himself and to develop his own interpretation of the data.

For purposes of checking the comparative validity of the technique used to assign children to this program versus the reading reinforced technique, one should first consider all of those children who made more than normal gain on the test administered at the end of the year and then see to what extent their "reading reinforced" test stanine would have predicted such excellent progress. Recall that normal gain, as used in this paper, means that the child's stanine would remain the same on the second test in the spring as on the first test in the fall. Those showing an actual loss would have negative stanine differences, while those who had gained more than the amount to be expected over the instructional period would show positive deviations.

FINDINGS

Nine children, or 26 per cent of the total group, showed positive deviations,—that is, gained more than one would expect in the period

68 | VALIDITY AND PREDICTION STUDIES

School Year 1969-70   Grade 3

Form D: Reinforced Administration

(Scatter plot matrix: Form C: Regular Administration (vertical, stanines 1-9) vs Form D: Reinforced Administration (horizontal, stanines 1-9))

Form C \ Form D	1	2	3	4	5	6	7	8	9	STANINE
9										
8										
7						4				1
6					23	1, 20	33		2	5
5					7	8, 19, 32	5	35		6
4					21, 29	3, 17, 22, 24, 25, 34, 36	6, 13, 16, 18, 26, 30, 31	11		17
3						10	15	14		3
2						28				1
1										
STANINE					4	14	11	3	1	33

FIGURE 8-1

Reading vs. Reading Reinforced Stanines Compared for Title 1 Cases in a Remedial Reading Program, Leominster, Massachusetts.

of instruction. These are Cases #6, 10, 15, 21, 24, 28, 33, 34, and 36. The results from the administration of the three forms of the *Metropolitan Reading Test* for these nine cases are shown in Table 8-1. All nine also showed gains on the reading reinforced test; seven showed more than normal gains,—that is, two or more stanine levels. Two showed gains of only one stanine under reinforcement, which must be considered within the normal limit. Thus, one can say that for seven of these nine cases the data suggest that real remedial problems did exist and the remedial program did seem to be successful.

Of the twenty-two cases shown in Figure 8-2 as falling within the mid-stanine band, nine showed gains of one stanine as compared to the

VALIDITY AND PREDICTION STUDIES | 69

	Spring: Form B									
	1	2	3	4	5	6	7	8	9	STANINE ←
9										
8										
7						4				1
6 (Fall: Form C)						1 2 / 20 23		33		5
5					7 19 / 32 35	5	8			6
4		25	26	30	3 16 / 29	11 13 / 17 18 / 22 31	6 21 / 24	34	36		17
3					14	15	10				3
2							28				1
1										
STANINE ↑		2	1	4	11	12	2	1		33

FIGURE 8-2

Pre- and Post-test Results in National Stanines Appropriate for the Time of Year for Grade Three Pupils in a Remedial Reading Program in Leominster, Massachusetts, Taking Metropolitan Elementary Reading in the Fall and Spring of 1969-70.

normal gain expected for the period of instruction, represented by a zero deviation. These data are summarized in Table 8-2. Conservatively, gains of less than two stanines should not be considered meaningful, but one can certainly say of these cases that the chances are better than even that the program was successful, if only moderately so. Note that all but one of these nine cases showed a gain of more than one stanine level under conditions of reinforcement. Note also, however, that the two highest stanines earned on the pre-test were stanines of five, or just average performance according to national norms, while on the post-test all but one were achieving a five or better.

TABLE 8-1
Metropolitan Reading Test Results in National Stanines for Children Who Gained Two or More Stanines on the Post-test. Leominster, Massachusetts, Remedial Reading Program—Grade Three.

Case #	Pre-Test Form C	Reading Reinforced Test-Form D	Post-Test Form B	Deviation Pre- to Post-Test
6	4	7	6	3
10	3	6	6	3
15	3	7	5	2
21	4	5	6	2
24	4	6	6	2
28	2	6	6	4
33	6	7	8	2
34	4	6	7	3
36	4	6	7	3

TABLE 8-2
Metropolitan Reading Test Results in National Stanines for Children Who Gained One Stanine Only on the Post-test. Leominster, Massachusetts, Remedial Reading Program—Grade Three.

Case #	Pre-Test Form C	Reading Reinforced Test-Form D	Post-Test Form B	Deviation Pre- to Post-Test
5	5	7	6	1
8	5	6	6	1
11	4	8	5	1
13	4	7	5	1
14	3	8	4	1
17	4	6	5	1
18	4	7	5	1
22	4	6	5	1
31	4	7	5	1

Of those children who did *not* show more than typical gain on the final test (Table 8-3), two cases actually showed a loss of two stanines. The reinforced testing showed that the two cases were potential reading disabled children and were correctly considered to be good risks. Child #25 showed a gain of two stanines under reinforcement and Child #26 had a gain of three stanines. It would seem that the corrective program not only did nothing for these two children in improving their reading skills, but there was an actual diminution in the success with which they attacked the reading problem as measured by Metropolitan. Anecdotal comments of the teachers indicate that these two children had problems beyond the special reading teacher's role or function to solve. For example, one child was from a broken home, had a short attention span, and showed a tendency to become aggressive when corrected in class. Obviously, more than corrective instruction in reading was needed in this instance. The other child was a Puerto Rican who spoke little English initially and was very shy. It appears likely that this child's problem was not really a remedial problem in reading, but one of bilingualism, with English being to him a foreign language.

In Table 8-3 there are fifteen cases where the post-test showed no gain in stanine or an absolute loss (four cases, #4, #25, #26, and #30). Also, of these fifteen cases, four showed no gain at all under reinforcement and one actually showed a loss. It is a common experience of those who have used this technique that most children do show some gain under reinforcement unless they are already reading up to capacity. To put this another way, it seems evident that a relatively small proportion of any total school population is reading up to its potential, if this potential is considered to be measured when the reading task is reinforced by hearing. However, seven of these cases showed substantial gains, that is, gains of two or more stanines under reinforcement. From that point of view, their performance on the post-test must be considered to be disappointing. In other words, they were selected by the teachers and school principals as cases needing remedial help and this

TABLE 8-3

Metropolitan Reading Test Results in National Stanines for Children Who Showed No Increase in Stanines on the Post-test. Leominster Massachusetts, Remedial Reading Program—Grade Three.

Case #	Pre-Test Form C	Reading Reinforced Test-Form D	Post-Test Form B	Deviation Pre- to Post-Test
1	6	6	6	0
2	6	9	6	0
3	4	6	4	0
4	7	7	6	−1
7	5	5	5	−1
16	4	7	4	0
19	5	6	5	0
20	6	6	6	0
23	6	5	6	0
25	4	6	2	−2
26	4	7	2	−2
29	4	5	4	0
30	4	7	3	−1
32	5	6	5	0
35	5	8	5	0

72 | **VALIDITY AND PREDICTION STUDIES**

initial selection was supported by the reinforced technique, and yet the students did not show the expected gain at the end of the period of instruction.

Seven children in Table 8-3 showing no stanine gain on the post-test had achieved little or no gain on the reading reinforced test. On the basis of the reinforced technique, these children would not be considered good candidates for special reading help. Since they were average or above average on the pre-test in the first place, it might be assumed that they were placed in the special reading services program because it was thought that they might improve under individual instruction. The reports from the classroom teacher did, in fact, cite the need for individual attention for these children and indicated poor daily performance in the regular classroom. The remedial reading teacher's comments indicated further problems, many well beyond the range of competence of the staff—visual difficulties, bilingualism, emotional disturbance, etc.

Table 8-4 presents still another look at these data. Included are thirteen cases making stanine gains of three or more on the reinforced test in the fall. In other words, these are the cases who would have been most likely to have been selected if the reinforced data were the sole basis for selection. Of the thirteen, four made substantial gains in the spring testing program, justifying their selection from the point of view

TABLE 8-4

Metropolitan Reading Test Results in National Stanines for Children Making Gains of Three or More Stanines Under Conditions of Reinforcement. Leominster, Massachusetts, Remedial Reading Program —Grade Three.

Case #	Pre-Test Form C	Reading Reinforced Test-Form D	Post-Test Form B	Deviation Pre- to Post-Test
2	6	9	6	0
6	4	7	6	2
10	3	6	6	3
13	4	7	5	1
14	3	8	4	1
15	3	7	5	2
16	4	7	4	0
18	4	7	5	1
26	4	7	2	−2
28	2	6	6	4
30	4	7	3	−1
31	4	7	5	1
11	4	8	5	1

of the reading reinforced technique. Five additional cases made gains of one stanine or, in other words, gained one stanine more than the normal progress to be expected of them during the course of the school year. This leaves four cases, each with one of the special problems mentioned, where the gain was no more than normal, or there was an actual loss as compared to fall testing.

In short, in Table 8-4 we see that nine of thirteen cases, or about 70 per cent, would have been considered very good prospects on the basis of the reinforced technique alone. In view of the extenuating circumstances, who can say that the four apparent failures were not appropriately included also?

SUMMARY

The reading reinforced technique appears to be a generally successful method of selecting students for special reading services; this does not negate the value of the teachers' recommendations, but one supplements the other. However, another year of experimentation on a larger scale should produce a more in-depth evaluation.

Reference

Durost, W. N. *Manual for interpreting Metropolitan achievement tests.* New York: Harcourt, Brace, and World, 1962.

Questions on the Crowley and Ellis article.
1. One of the criteria for selection used in this study was "mental ability within the normal range." What is meant by this?
2. Exactly what do the authors mean by "cross validation?"
3. State exactly what Figure 8-1 tells us about student number 35. About student number 7.
4. State exactly what Figure 8-2 tells us about student number 4. About student number 28.
5. How would you go about testing the null hypothesis that the children of this sample did not gain significantly between their Form C and Form D Metropolitan Reading Test scores?
6. In summarizing Table 8-4, the authors refer to "extenuating circumstances." To what might they be referring?

9

DETERMINING THE VALIDITY AND RELIABILITY OF AN ATTITUDINAL INSTRUMENT

Michael J. Savage
Salem State College
Salem, Massachusetts

BACKGROUND

A study, (Savage, 1971) was undertaken to determine if there were any differences in attitudes between school administrators and special educators toward exceptional children. In order to complete this study it was necessary to develop a comprehensive attitudinal scale for the 11 areas of exceptional children: trainable mentally retarded; educable mentally retarded; emotionally disturbed; hard of hearing; deaf; partially sighted; blind; speech impaired; learning disabilities; orthopedically handicapped; and chronic health problems.

The purpose of this article is to describe the methods used by Savage to determine the reliability and content validity of the attitudinal instrument prepared especially for this study. It is certainly true that the results of any empirical piece of research are only as good as the instruments used to collect the data. Perhaps, then, techniques such as presented here will be both a reminder and a guide to educators wishing to assure that the results of their attitudinal research projects are not biased by invalid and unreliable data collecting instruments.

METHODOLOGIES AND RESULTS

Selection of scale and items. Before deciding upon the type of scale to use several variables had to be considered. First, it had to be one that could include a sufficient number of discriminating statements for each of the 11 areas of exceptional children. Second, it had to be concise and relatively easy to complete. Third, it had to yield reliable information about the respondents' agreement or disagreement toward a particular psychological trait. Finally, it had to be a scale that could be easily constructed and developed to meet these foregoing requirements.

According to Oppenheim (1966, pp. 133-142) the type of instrument that satisfies these requirements best is the Likert type scale. This is an attitudinal scale so designed that each statement is followed by multiple-choice forced response categories on an agree-disagree horizontal continuum. Respondents indicate their attitudes toward each statement by selecting the response appropriate for them.

It was determined that a scale of 55 items, that is, five statements for each of the 11 areas of exceptional children would be sufficient for this instrument. In order to select the best items for the final scale an item analysis was conducted so as to determine which items were able to discriminate between people who have positive attitudes toward a particular psychological object from those who have negative attitudes (Edwards, 1957; Oppenheim, 1966). In order to make these determinations a number of statements had to be selected from the original pool of over 500 items. It was decided to choose 10 items from each area, 110 in all, so that the item analysis could be undertaken.

The 110 items were selected by three subject matter experts on the basis of the following criteria. First, Edwards and Kilpatrick's (1948) informal criteria for the editing of statements to be used in an attitudinal scale were followed. Second, the relevancy of each item to a particular area of exceptional children was weighted. Third, the item had to reflect an attitude toward a particular group of exceptional children.

Following the selection of the 110 items the five point forced response weighted scale for each statement was decided upon. A five is arrived at by strongly agreeing with a positive statement or strongly disagreeing with a negative statement. A four is arrived at by agreeing with a positive statement or disagreeing with a negative statement. A three is arrived at by being undecided about a statement. A two is arrived at by disagreeing with a positive statement or agreeing with a negative statement. Finally, a one is arrived at by strongly disagreeing with a positive statement or strongly agreeing with a negative statement. The range of possible total scores for this preliminary scale was 110 to 550. Each item was then randomly assigned to the instrument in order to offset any kind of a response set (Edwards, 1957; Oppenheim, 1966).

Item analysis. Oppenheim has stated, "Ideally, the item analysis should take place by correlating each item with some reliable outside criterion of the attitude it is supposed to measure and retaining only those items with the highest correlations" (p. 138). This external standard is usually not available. Therefore, for the time being, the best measures of the attitudes concerned are the 110 items. The purpose of the item analysis was to purify the group of items so that they were consistent and homogeneous. According to Anastasi (1969, pp. 158-184), by utilizing an item analysis in advance, high reliability and validity can be built into the instrument. Consequently, by conducting the item analysis or more specifically, item discrimination, it is possible to retain only those items with the highest point biserial correlations with the total score. Further, the scale is shortened and the reliability and validity are increased.

Therefore, it was decided to determine point biserial correlation coefficients for each item with the total score and keep only those items with the highest correlations. That this would satisfy the validity of the scale (Oppenheim, 1966), was the prevailing reason for such a choice.

The preliminary instrument of 110 items was administered to a pilot group of 50 school administrators and 50 special educators. Subsequently, each of the statements on all 100 instruments was scored and totalled. Next, all 100 instruments were placed in rank order, from the lowest to the highest total score regardless of their group membership.

The item discrimination process was initiated by taking the third of the instruments with the highest total scores and the third with the lowest total scores from this group. (Anastasi, 1969; Edwards, 1957; Oppenheim, 1966.) These two groups now provide criterion groups in terms of evaluating the 110 individual statements.

The next step was to develop a work sheet, from which to keypunch the data. The 66 individual (high third-low third) were placed in order of their scores from lowest to highest. Every individual's responses to each of the 110 items was recorded in the appropriate numbered column to the right of their total score. These were marked "0" for a negative attitude; "1" for a positive attitude; and "2" for undecided. When this was completed, the one item from each of the 11 areas of exceptional children with the most undecided responses, was eliminated, leaving only 99 items. Next the investigator proceeded down each column, starting with item 1 eradicating any undecided responses "2" and alternately replacing them with either a positive "1" or negative response "0." The reason for this was that the item analysis was being conducted to select those items that best discriminates, favorably or unfavorably, between extreme groups.

The final step in the item analysis was the actual correlation between the items and the total score, using the point biserial correlation. A point biserial correlation delineates a measure of relationship between a continuous variable, total score, and a dichotomous variable assumed to be an actual continuous psychological variable, positive or negative attitude (Ferguson, 1966, p. 239). This dichotomous variable may be thought of as extending along a horizontal continuum of varying degrees of positive to negative affect toward some psychological concept. In this particular situation the individuals had two choices with which to respond positively and two options with which to respond negatively toward each statement. However, for statistical computation this continuum was made a discrete dichotomous variable, a positive "1" or negative attitude "0."

VALIDITY AND PREDICTION STUDIES | 77

TABLE 9-1
Discrimination Indices Obtained by an Item Analysis Employing the Point-Biserial Correlation (ypbi) Method

TMR		EMR		Emot. Dist.		Part. Sighted		Blind		Learn. Dis.		Hard. Hear.		Deaf		Sp. Imp.		Orth. Handi.		Ch. Health Prob.	
Item	ypbi	Item	ypbi	Item	ypbi	Item	ypbi	Item	ypbi	Item	ypbi	Item	ypbi	Item	ypbi	Item	ypbi	Item	ypbi	Item	ypbi
29	.2761	5	.4814	19	.4065	b 1	.6468	15	.4241	3	.4234	b12	.4687	6	.1118	b 7	.5557	4	.3247	b 2	.4527
b38	.5256	b10	.5220	b33	.6491	b 8	.3451	17	.4893	9	.4058	b13	.4083	b11	.4593	14	.3151	b16	.4542	a14	Omit
b47	.4294	a13	Omit	34	.1461	b24	.2933	18	.3203	b20	.4588	b21	.3680	40	.4436	a24	Omit	b27	.5110	b22	.4473
a51	Omit	b23	.5136	48	.3797	25	.2414	b28	.5896	b26	.4719	31	.2405	b43	.5246	b36	.5430	b35	.5619	b51	.5291
b65	.7075	b30	.5599	b49	.4918	b45	.2757	b37	.5172	b32	.4850	b39	.3533	a54	Omit	b53	.6300	41	.4000	69	.1605
b66	.4707	b42	.4883	b50	.5848	46	.2603	44	.3680	54	.1731	55	.1689	52	.0502	57	.2779	77	.2091	56	.4069
75	0.0	61	.4193	b63	.5098	b60	.6419	b59	.5361	b58	.7332	64	.0352	b67	.5205	68	.4782	b62	.4452	b81	.2516
78	.1398	b70	.5930	a71	Omit	a70	Omit	b71	.5983	b72	.5055	b76	.4159	74	.1343	b80	.6247	b73	.5196	b86	.4812
b82	.7444	93	.3354	b85	.4610	78	.1398	b84	.5729	89	.4292	87	.3304	b83	.5678	b90	.7999	a96	Omit	88	.0566
92	.0840	95	.0971	98	.4594	91	.0408	a105	Omit	a104	Omit	a101	Omit	b94	.6041	96	.3965	97	.0852	99	.1139

Note—Item numbers were changed following the elimination of an item from each category on original scale.
[a] Items omitted retain original numbers from preliminary scale.
[b] Items retained for final instrument.

According to Remmers (1954) when conducting an item analysis one should establish a minimum standard of discriminating power for selecting items "... and in no case to select items with discriminating power less than the minimum" (p. 132). Therefore, only those five items with the highest discrimination values as determined by the point biserial correlation coefficients (r_{pbi}), were to be retained in each of the 11 areas of exceptional children. Garrett (1958, p. 368) considers an item with a validity index of .20 as satisfactory and one with .40 as highly valid.

An inspection of Table 9-1 indicates that 89% or 49 out of 55 items retained had discrimination indices above .40. The lowest discrimination index of the remaining six items was .25. Thus all items met the Garrett (1958) criterion and these 55 items appear to make the total instrument a valid one for differentiating those with favorable or unfavorable attitudes toward exceptional children.

Estimation of reliability. According to Van Calen (1966) "... a scale is reliable if it consistently yields the same results when repeated measurements are taken of the same subjects under the same conditions" (p. 315). Therefore, reliability means the extent to which the scale or instrument agrees with itself.

Of the three major types of reliability this investigation was concerned specifically with that labeled as stability (American Psychological Association, 1966). Measures of this kind (coefficients of stability) involve retesting with the same form of the instrument following a length of time, hence the procedure has been called test-retest reliability. This particular approach implies that the trait being measured is stable, and that between administrations of the instrument the individuals or group have not experienced anything which may seriously affect the characteristics measured.

The reliability of the final scale was determined during the summer of 1970 by administering it to 51 graduate students in special education at Boston College. The attitudinal scale was administered at the end of class time on two separate occasions, one week apart.

The scales were then scored as before except that instead of 110 items there were now 55 items and the possible score ranged from 275 to 55. Worksheets were then constructed for estimating not only the reliability of the entire instrument, but for each of the 11 areas of exceptionality. The computations of the reliability were calculated using the raw score formula for computing the Pearson Product Moment Correlation Coefficient (r).

$$r = \frac{N\Sigma XY - \Sigma X \Sigma Y}{\sqrt{[N\Sigma X^2 - (\Sigma X)^2][N\Sigma Y^2 - (\Sigma Y)^2]}}$$

VALIDITY AND PREDICTION STUDIES | 79

TABLE 9-2

Pearson Product Moment Correlation Estimate of
the Reliability of the Entire Instrument

	Pretest	Post-test
N	51	51
X	225.21	225.68
SD	16.66	17.04
	r = .9048	

TABLE 9-3

Pearson Product Moment Correlation Estimates of the Reliability for Each Group of Items Representing Each of the Eleven Areas of Exceptional Children

Area	Items	$\bar{X}$ Pretest	$\bar{X}$ Post-test	r
Trainable Mentally Retarded	3, 12, 18, 44, 53	21.88	21.76	.7252
Educable Mentally Retarded	8, 19, 33, 37, 48	21.64	21.60	.7515
Emotionally Disturbed	4, 9, 23, 45, 52	21.25	21.09	.7946
Partially Sighted	2, 7, 24, 31, 46	20.21	20.15	.6360
Blind	1, 17, 34, 36, 42	20.76	20.60	.8260
Learning Disabilities	14, 21, 30, 39, 55	18.41	18.58	.5860
Hard of Hearing	13, 22, 32, 43, 50	20.27	20.49	.6060
Deaf	6, 10, 11, 16, 27	20.80	20.86	.7810
Speech Impairments	25, 29, 40, 41, 47	20.43	20.17	.8060
Orthopedically Handicapped	5, 15, 20, 28, 54	20.41	20.23	.7640
Chronic Health Problems	26, 35, 38, 49, 51	19.41	19.64	.7113

A brief inspection of Tables 9-2 and 9-3 indicates that not only is the entire instrument reliable, but each of the sub-groups of items that make up the test is also reliable. The investigator is well aware of the foibles that are inherent in the test-retest procedures (Anastasi, 1969, p. 80; Cronbach, 1970, p. 177). However, in estimating the initial reliability of the instrument sufficient time was allowed between the first and second testings to offset, in part at least, the practice effect and any other carryover effects. Therefore, this instrument appears to be both valid and reliable for the purposes of the research that was conducted.

References

Anastasi, A. *Psychological testing. (3rd ed.)* Toronto: Collier-MacMillan, Limited, 1969.

American Psychological Association. *Standard for educational and psychological tests and manuals.* Washington, D.C. Author, 1966.

Cronbach, L. J. *Essentials of psychological testing. (3rd ed.)* New York: Harper & Row, 1970.

Edwards, A. L. & Kilpatrick, F. P. A techniques for the construction of attitude scales. *Journal of Applied Psychology,* 1948, 32, 374-384.

Edwards, A. L. *Techniques of attitude scale construction.* New York: Appleton-Century-Crofts, 1957.

Ferguson, G. A. *Statistical analysis in psychology and education. (2nd ed.)* New York: McGraw-Hill, 1966.

Garrett, H. E. *Statistics in psychology and education (5th ed.)* New York: Longmans, Green and Company, 1958.

Oppenheim, A. N. *Questionaire design and attitude measurement.* New York: Basic Books, 1966.

Remmers, H. H. *Introduction to opinion and attitude measurements.* New York: Harper & Brothers, 1954.

Savage, M. J. *An investigation of the differences in attitudes between and among school administrators and special education personnel toward exceptional children.* Unpublished doctoral dissertation, Boston College, 1971.

Questions for the Savage Study:
1. The author's criterion groups for determining item discrimination were the 33 instruments with the highest total score and the 33 with the lowest. What was his rationale for not using all 100 instruments?
2. In what other way(s) could the author have determined the item discrimination index of each item?
3. The author refers to his reliability coefficients as coefficients of stability. What is the limitation of a coefficient of stability? What other reliability coefficients are there?
5. Distinguish between a Likert-type attitudinal scale and a Thurstone-type attitudinal scale. Did the authors use either one? Explain.
6. What limitations did the author impose by his method of dichotomizing the results of his attitudinal instrument?

10

CAN SCORES OBTAINED FROM THE SLOSSON INTELLIGENCE TEST BE USED WITH AS MUCH CONFIDENCE AS SCORES OBTAINED FROM THE STANFORD-BINET INTELLIGENCE SCALE?

ROBERT J. ARMSTRONG
Salem State College
Salem, Massachusetts

and

JOHN A. JENSEN
Boston College
Chestnut Hill, Massachusetts

PURPOSE

An individual intelligence test requiring no specialized training and which takes only 15 to 20 minutes to administer and score would be of great value, particularly to counselors and other specialized personnel who are spending a large portion of their time administering the more technical tests such as the S-B. Thus, it was the purpose of this study to determine the validity of the Slosson Intelligence Test (SIT), using the Stanford-Binet intelligence Scale (S-B), Form L-M, as the validity criterion.

METHOD

The sample consisted of 724 students (ages 6 to 14) enrolled in 10 public school systems in northeastern Massachusetts. Each student was administered both an SIT and an S-B within a two week period of time.

The tests were administered using various combinations of personnel. The administrators were classified in three ways: professionals, trainees and teachers. *Professionals* were highly trained and experienced personnel in the field of testing (limited to 3 in this study). *Trainees* were part-time graduate students (mostly teachers) who were enrolled in a course concerned with administering, scoring and interpreting the S-B and who had administered numerous S-B's under super-

82 | VALIDITY AND PREDICTION STUDIES

vision before administering any tests in this study. The *Teachers* involved had no knowledge concerning the administration of the S-B.

Pearson-Product Moment correlation coefficients between S-B and SIT scores were computed for each of the following 21 categories.

1. *Overall*—for all 724 subjects;
2–10. *Age Levels*—for each age level separately (6-14);
11. *Male*—for all male subjects;
12. *Female*—for all female subjects;
13. *Same Administrator*—for both tests;
14. *Different Administrator*—for each test;
15. *Professional Administrator*—for both tests, but not necessarily the same administrator;
16. *Trainee Administrator*—for both tests, but not necessarily the same administrator;
17. *Professional and Teacher Administrators*—S-B by a professional and the SIT by a teacher, neither was aware the other test was given or was going to be given;
18. *S-B Administered First;*
19. *SIT Administered First;*
20. *Same Day*—when both tests were administered on the same day;
21. *Different Day*—when the administration of the second test was completed between one and 14 days after the first administration.

Also, the mean absolute difference between IQ scores from the two scales was computed for each of the preceding categories.

RESULTS

Table 10-1 shows that the overall Pearson Product Moment correlation between the S-B and the SIT was .92. Also, the range of correlations for the nine *Age Levels* (6-14) was from .90 *(Ages 6 and 8)* to .95 *(Age 13)*. All correlations were significant beyond the .001 probability level. These correlations approximate those reported by Slosson (1963) for these *Age Levels* (.94 to .98).

Table 10-2 presents the findings concerning additional categories which were either not reported or not substantially validated by Slosson: (1) *Sex;* (2) *Same* and *Different Administrators;* (3) *Administrator Status;* (4) *Order* of test administration; and (5) *Time Lapse* between the first and second administration. The range of correlations for these 11 sub-categoreis was from .92 *(Both Trainees)* to .94 *(Professional and Teachers)*. All correlations were significant beyond the .001 probability level.

The standard deviations in both Tables 10-1 and 10-2 are large when compared to the standard deviation of 16 for the S-B itself, and have perhaps produced somewhat inflated correlation coefficients. However, what is more important than their size, is the correspondence of the S-B and SIT standard deviations.

Since Slosson's purpose was to construct an abbreviated form of the S-B, these high validity coefficients (Tables 10-1 and 10-2) are, in a sense, reliability coefficients. At any rate, the fact that the correlation between the S-B and the SIT approximates the reliability of the S-B itself, indicates that the tests appear to be measuring the same thing. It should be noted that the results of this study indicate a statistical relationship between IQ scores from these two tests, and should not be interpreted as meaning that a score from one test can be substituted for a score for the other without regard to what is being measured by the individual or respective tests (Lindquist, 1964; Wesman, 1958).

Further evidence concerning the comparability of scores from these two tests is revealed in Table 10-1. Note that the *Overall* average absolute IQ score point difference between the two tests was 5.46, which is approximately the same as the standard error of measurement of 5 IQ score points of the S-B. The range of average absolute IQ score point difference for the 20 sub-categories (Tables 10-1 and 10-2) was from 4.03 *(Professionals* and *Teachers)* to 5.88 *(Age 9).*

TABLE 10-1

Cross Validation of Slosson's Findings
Means, Standard Deviations, Correlations and Average Differences of IQ Scores of the Stanford-Binet Intelligence Scale, Form L-M, and the Slosson Intelligence Test

Category	N	Mean S-B	Mean SIT	Standard Deviation S-B	Standard Deviation SIT	r*	Average Absolute IQ Difference
Overall	724	106.44	107.28	18.20	19.23	.92	5.46
Age 6	77	102.52	102.88	17.36	16.73	.90	5.84
Age 7	88	109.01	109.80	18.19	18.64	.92	5.42
Age 8	85	110.67	112.26	16.57	17.48	.90	5.75
Age 9	83	104.83	106.45	16.45	18.61	.91	5.88
Age 10	87	103.48	104.26	18.64	18.81	.92	5.52
Age 11	80	104.25	105.00	18.99	20.62	.94	5.28
Age 12	72	107.47	108.83	18.05	19.95	.93	5.28
Age 13	80	108.38	108.83	18.60	20.58	.95	4.68
Age 14	72	107.13	106.88	19.12	20.11	.93	5.61

*<.001 (All correlation coefficients are significant beyond the .001 level)

VALIDITY AND PREDICTION STUDIES

TABLE 10-2

Additional Findings of This Study
Means, Standard Deviations, Correlations and Average Differences of IQ
Scores of the Stanford-Binet Intelligence Scale, Form L-M,
and the Slosson Intelligence Test

Category	N	Mean S-B	Mean SIT	Standard Deviation S-B	Standard Deviation SIT	r*	Average Absolute IQ Difference
Male	379	106.00	106.82	18.81	19.77	.93	5.20
Female	345	106.92	107.78	17.49	18.72	.91	5.77
Same Administrator	49;	108.24	109.37	18.87	18.96	.93	5.50
Different Administrator	233	102.74	102.87	16.03	19.19	.92	5.42
Admin. Status Both Professionals	304	100.90	101.30	15.24	18.58	.93	5.48
Admin. Status Both Trainees	368	110.57	112.02	19.21	18.66	.92	5.62
Admin. Status Professionals and Teachers	52	109.52	108.65	18.20	17.92	.94	4.03
Order S-B First	440	106.50	107.96	17.34	18.45	.93	5.68
Order SIT First	284	106.33	106.22	19.44	20.46	.93	5.68
2nd Administration Same Day	401	104.99	105.75	17.68	18.22	.93	5.14
2nd Administration 1-14 Days	253	111.34	113.64	18.52	19.82	.93	5.64

*$<.001$ (All correlation coefficients are significant beyond the .001 level)

CONCLUSIONS

The results indicate that for this study consisting of 724 subjects, the SIT appears to be measuring the same thing as the S-B. The results of each of the sub-categoreis (age, sex, administrator's status, order of administration and time interval between tests) are in close agreement with the overall study findings concerning both the correlation between the two tests and their average absolute IQ score point differences. Thus, the findings suggest that the SIT can be used as a valid screening and retesting substitute for the S-B and provide: (1) an opportunity for more individual intelligence tests to be given; (2) a source of additional test administrators; and (3) more time for specialized personnel to devote to their other responsibilities.

Although the results of this study are highly favorable, additional research is needed such as studies of the validity of the Slosson in making judgments concerning placement of children in special education classes and placement of children in classes for the gifted.

REFERENCES
Lindquist, E. F. "Equaling Scores on Non-parallel Tests." *Journal of Educational Measurement.* 1964, 1, 5-9.
Wesman, A. G. "Comparability vs. Equivalence of Test Scores." *Test Service Bulletin,* No. 53. New York: The Psychological Corporation, 1958.
Slosson, Richard L. *Slosson Intelligence Test for Children and Adults.* East Aurora, New York: Slosson Publications, 1963.

Questions on the Armstrong and Jensen article.
1. The overall study sample was broken down into 20 sub-categories such as age and sex. What additional sub-categories do you think need to be investigated?
2. In the RESULTS section, discuss what is meant by the statement, "Since Slosson's purpose was to construct an abbreviated form of the S-B, these high validity coefficients (Tables 10-1 and 10-2) are, in a sense, reliability coefficients."
3. In the RESULTS section, discuss what is meant by the statement, "The Standard deviations in both Tables 10-1 and 10-2 are large when compared to the standard deviation of 16 for the S-B itself, and have perhaps produced somewhat inflated correlation coefficients. However, what is more important than their size, is the correspondence of the S-B and SIT standard deviations."
4. In Tables 10-1 and 10-2, explain what is meant by the statement, "all correlation coefficients are significant beyond the .001 probability level."
5. If the coefficient of correlation between two variables is significant, is it possible that there is a significant difference between the means of the two variables? Explain your answer.

11

THE SLOSSON INTELLIGENCE TEST: IMPLICATIONS FOR READING SPECIALISTS

ROBERT J. ARMSTRONG and ROBERT F. MOONEY
Salem State College
Salem, Massachusetts

INTRODUCTION

The intelligence test is one of the primary evaluative instruments used by specialized personnel such as reading supervisors. This is true whether the reason for evaluation is prognostic or diagnostic. Since decisions resulting from evaluation often have a great influence on the present and future welfare of students, high standards concerning reliability and validity must be applied in the selection of test instruments. When IQ scores are used as one of the criteria in evaluation, specialized personnel such as reading supervisors usually prefer to use scores obtained from a recently administered individual test of intelligence such as the *Stanford-Binet* (S-B) *Intelligence Scale,* Form L-M. Unfortunately, individual intelligence tests are time consuming in that they require an average administration time of approximately one hour and require specialized training to administer and score. Thus, there is a need for a valid individual test of mental ability, requiring no specialized training, which could be quickly administered and easily scored.

In 1963, Richard L. Slosson constructed the *Slosson Intelligence Test* (SIT), sometimes referred to as the *Short Intelligence Test.* The purpose of its author was to construct an abbreviated form of the *Stanford-Binet Intelligence Scale* (S-B), Form L-M, which could be used as a screening and retesting instrument and thus provide: (1) an opportunity for more students to receive individual intelligence tests; and (2) more released time for specialized personnel to devote to their other responsibilities.

The SIT is an individual test of intelligence for both children and adults, requiring no specialized training, which takes only fifteen to twenty minutes to administer and score. A test-retest reliability coefficient of .97 and a standard error of measurement of 4.3 IQ score points is reported by Slosson for 139 subjects ranging from four to fifty years old.

The *Stanford-Binet Intelligence Scale* (S-B), Form L-M, was used as the criterion for establishing the concurrent validity of the *Slosson*

Intelligence Test (SIT). Slosson reports correlation coefficients between these two tests ranging from .90 through .98 (median .96) for subjects whose ages ranged from four to eighteen and above. Moreover, he reports an average absolute IQ score difference of 5.2 between the two tests (Slosson, 1963).

PURPOSE

It was the purpose of this study to determine the validity of the *Slosson Intelligence Test* (SIT), using the *Stanford-Binet Intelligence Scale* (S-B), Form L-M as the validity criterion. More specifically, the purpose of this study was to answer the following two questions.
1. Can scores obtained from the SIT be used with as much confidence as scores obtained from the S-B, when both tests have been administered by a test specialist?
2. Can scores obtained from the SIT administered by a teacher be used with as much confidence as scores obtained from the S-B administered by a test specialist?

For purposes of this study, *test specialists* were defined as experienced personnel in the field of testing, and qualified to administer the S-B. *Teachers* were defined as personnel with no knowledge concerning the administration of the S-B.

METHOD

The study used, for its testing sample, a total of 204 students, ages six to fourteen, enrolled in ten public school systems in northeastern Massachusetts. The test administrators for the study consisted of four test specialists and ten teachers from these same ten school systems.

To determine if scores obtained from the SIT can be used with as much confidence as scores obtained from the S-B when both tests have been administered by a test specialist, 152 students were administered both an S-B and an SIT by test specialists within a two week period of time. In order to obtain comparative results and to avoid bias: (1) each test was administered first an equal number of times; (2) in half of the cases both tests were administered by the same person; and (3) for the other half of the cases, two different administrators were used.

To determine if scores obtained from the SIT administered by a teacher can be used with as much confidence as scores obtained from the S-B administered by a test specialist, fifty-two students were administered an SIT by a teacher, and an S-B by a test specialist. In order to obtain comparative results and also to avoid bias: (1) each test was administered first an equal number of times; and (2) neither administrator was aware that a second test had been or was going to be administered.

The teachers in the second experiment were provided an opportunity to teach themselves how to administer and score the SIT. The teachers indicated that the directions were written clearly, and reported an average self-instruction time of approximately thirty minutes. However, an opportunity was provided these teachers to ask questions concerning the SIT before they administered any tests in this study.

The same statistical treatment was applied separately to both of the preceding experiments, and was accomplished in the following manner. First, using the Pearson-Product Moment formula, a coefficient of correlation was computed between the S-B and SIT IQ scores. Then, the average absolute IQ score point difference was computed, where average absolute IQ score point difference is defined as the average absolute IQ score point differences between individual's S-B and SIT scores.

RESULTS

The Pearson-Product Moment correlation coefficients between S-B and SIT IQ scores are reported in Table 11-1. The table reveals correlation coefficients of: (1) .93 when both tests were administered by test specialists; and (2) .94 when the S-B's were administered by test specialists and the SIT's by teachers.

TABLE 11-1

Means, Standard Deviations, Correlations, and Average Absolute IQ Score Differences for the Stanford-Binet (S-B) and Slosson (SIT) Intelligence Test Scores

	Testing Specialist (S-B)	Testing Specialist (SIT)	Testing Specialist (S-B)	Teacher (SIT)
N	152.00	152.00	52.00	52.00
X	100.90	101.30	109.51	108.65
SD	15.24	18.19	18.58	17.91
r		.93		.94
Average IQ Difference		5.46		4.40

Since Slosson's purpose was to construct an abbreviated form of the S-B, these high validity coefficients are, in a sense, reliability coefficients. At any rate, the fact that the correlation between the S-B and the SIT approximates the reliability of the S-B itself indicates that the tests appear to be measuring the same thing. It should be noted that the results of this study indicate a statistical relationship between IQ scores from these two tests, and should not be interpreted as meaning that a score for one test can be substituted for a score for the other without regard to what is being measured by the individual or respective tests (Lindquist, 1964, Wesman, 1958).

Additionally, the average IQ score differences were computed for both experiments. The average absolute IQ score point differences reported in Table 11-1 were 5.46 (both testing specialists) and 4.40 (testing specialists and teachers). These average differences are approximately the same as the standard error of measurement of five IQ score points of the S-B itself, and provides further evidence concerning the comparability of scores obtained from these two tests. That is, the average difference between these two tests was approximately the same as the difference one might expect from a test-retest scores of the S-B itself.

Because there is an average IQ score point difference between two tests, it does not necessarily follow that one of the tests is consistently yielding higher or lower scores. For example, in one situation the S-B might be ten points higher than the SIT while in another the SIT might be ten points higher than the S-B. In this example, the average IQ point difference is ten, but the means would be identical. This concept is also illustrated in Table 11-1, where close inspection reveals that the means and standard deviation in both experiments are remarkably consistent.

A graphic illustration of the relationship between S-B and SIT IQ scores is afforded by the scattergram shown in Figure 11-1. The plot shows the distributions of IQ scores obtained when the S-B's were administered by testing specialists and the SIT's were administered by teachers. Figure 11-1 serves to reinforce, by a graphic illustration, the close relationship between S-B and SIT scores previously indicated in Table 11-1 (r = .95; average IQ difference 4.40).

The average administration time for the S-B was 64 minutes, compared to 17 minutes for the SIT. Therefore, on an average administration of the S-B took approximately four times longer.

CONCLUSIONS

It appears from the results of this study that, for these students, scores obtained from the SIT administered by either a test specialist or

VALIDITY AND PREDICTION STUDIES

Teachers' Slosson (SIT) IQ's

Testing Specialists' Stanford-Binet IQ's	65-69	70-74	75-79	80-84	85-89	90-94	95-99	100-104	105-109	110-114	115-119	120-124	125-129	130-134	135-139	140-144	145-149	150-154	
150-154																I			1
145-149																			
140-144																I			1
135-139															I	I			2
130-134													I	II	I				4
125-129												II	I						4
120-124								I	II	II	II								7
115-119							I		I		I								3
110-114										II	I								3
105-109								I	II	II	I								6
100-104								IIII	I										6
95-99							I	II		I									4
90-94						II	II												4
85-89					II														2
80-84				I	I	I													3
75-59																			
70-74		I																	1
65-69	I																		1
	1	2		3	1	2	5	9	5	4	6	3	3	3	3	2			52

N = 52   r = .94   Average IQ Difference = 4.40

FIGURE 11-1

Correlation Scattergram Showing Relationship between Stanford-Binet IQ's as Obtained by Testing Specialists and Slosson IQ's as Obtained by Teachers

a teacher can be used with as much confidence as scores obtained from the S-B administered by a test specialist. The results reinforce Slosson's purposes for constructing the test; namely, to develop an abbreviated test that: (1) can be used as a valid screening and retesting instrument; (2) does not require specialized training to administer and score; and (3) can be administered in one-fourth of the time required of the S-B.

The intelligence test is one of the primary evaluation instruments used by specialized reading personnel such as directors, supervisors, and clinicians. This is true whether the reason for evaluation is prognostic, diagnostic, initial screening, or retesting. When scores are used as one of the criteria in evaluation, scores obtained from recently administered individual test of intelligence such as the S-B are preferred. Unfortunately, reading personnel, like other specialized personnel, are faced with a shortage of time and qualified personnel to administer the more technical tests. Thus, the results obtained when the S-B was administered by a test specialist and the SIT by a teacher should be of particular interest to reading supervisors since it provides them not only with a valid abbreviated test but also with an expanded source of test administrators. For example, classroom teachers and reading specialists not qualified to administer S-B's, could be used to administer the SIT. This additional source of test administrators will allow more individual intelligence tests to be given and allow specialized personnel more time for their other responsibilities.

Questions on the Armstrong and Mooney article.
1. Discuss the acceptability of the sample in terms of its size. Does it restrict the usage of the results of this study? If so, how would you have sampled?
2. How would you go about determining if the coefficients of correlation reported in Table 11-1 are significant?
3. The ages of the students in the study ranged from six to fourteen. What effect, if any, do you think this had on the coefficients of correlation?
4. Compare the terms *average absolute IQ score difference* and *standard error of measurement*.
5. In the INTRODUCTION section of the article, the authors reported that the reliability of the SIT was based on a population of 139 subjects, ages 4-50 (test-retest reliability coefficient .97; standard error of measurement 4.3). Discuss the validity of a reliability coefficient based on such a limited norming population.
6. Although the results of this study are favorable, it is obvious that additional research is needed comparing the SIT with the S-B and other IQ tests. List six studies which you feel need to be conducted.

12

THE INFLUENCE OF TEST TITLE ON TEST RESPONSE*

JOHN A. JENSEN and JOHN A. SCHMITT
Boston College
Chestnut Hill, Massachusetts

This study was designed to determine the extent to which responses to test items of the type frequently found in personality inventories would be influenced by the title associated with the test. The basic hypothesis was that subjects respond to the test title by developing a particular response set which will be reflected in the individual responses. An instrument was constructed and administered to eight treatment groups. Each administration differed primarily in the title each group's tests bore. The dependent variables were measures of the tendency to lie, respond defensively, answer carefully, and complete questions. Subjects tended to lie and respond more defensively to titled tests than to a test having no title and administered under nonthreatening conditions. All other comparisons were not statistically significant.

Considering the manner in which most personality tests are administered, particularly in schools and colleges, it is astonishing that no prior investigation of title-influence has been reported (at least to the knowledge of the writers). Most measurement textbooks caution students against the uncritical assumption that a test is actually measuring the construct implied by its title (Rothney, et al., 1959, pp. 122-131), but the possibility that test scores may be partly determined by the instrument's title is largely ignored.

INSTRUMENTATION

The basic instrument was constructed using items which contribute to L (lie), F (validity), and K (defensiveness against psychological weakness) scale scores on the Minnesota Multiphasic Personality Inventory (MMPI).[1]

Since responses to individual items may well be influenced by the context of items in which they are found (a problem related to the one under investigation), the writers assumed that responses to these items

*"Reprinted from Journal of Educational Measurement, Vol. 7, No. 4, Winter of 1970. Used by permission of the publisher and the authors."

out of the context of the entire MMPI might well deserve a special interpretation.[2] The objective, however, was not to relate findings from this investigation to the MMPI itself, rather, to the general class of instruments which contain items demanding information which, to the respondent, may appear personal and/or potentially damaging. In all, 106 items were selected.

Items of particular interest were those comprising the MMPI L-Scale, 15 items intended to provide evidence as to whether the subject is responding candidly to the instrument as a whole. High scores on the L-Scale indicate a tendency on the part of the subject to respond to items in a manner calculated to place himself in a favorable light. Items from the F-Scale were included to provide an indication of the care with which each subject responded to the entire test. It seemed worthwhile to include such a measure, since each subject might differ from others on this dimension, depending on the purpose he assumed the test was serving, and the assumed purpose could possibly be determined by the test's title.

Items from the K-Scale were included for two reasons. First, it was felt that they might differentiate among subjects responding to instruments supposed to be serving different purposes. While the psychological meaningfulness of K is at issue, it has been suggested that this scale represents an aspect of test-taking attitude. More specifically, K is often regarded as indicating "defensiveness against psychological weakness" (Hathaway & McKinley, 1951, p. 18). Second, even if K-Scale items did not serve to differentiate among groups of subjects supposedly responding to different instruments, at least they could serve to camouflage the items on the other scales.

A fourth measure was obtained for each subject by counting the number of "cannot decide" responses. As such, this variable was analogous to the (?) score employed with the MMPI.

Since the purpose of the study was to determine whether or not subjects respond differentially to instruments which differ only in their titles, titles were formulated in an effort to appear to tap a variety of areas about which college students might be concerned.

The titles used were:
1. The Boston College Psychological Adjustment Inventory
2. The Boston College Academic Potential Inventory
3. The Boston College Christian Character Inventory
4. The Boston College Social Desirability Inventory

2. Since there is evidence to indicate that item responses obtained to selected items isolated from the context of a personality inventory may not be comparable to those obtained within the context, the results of this research should not be considered applicable to the standardized complete form of the inventory.

5. The Boston College Political Inclination Inventory
6. The Boston College Attitude and Interest Inventory

Two control groups were employed. The first of these responded to a test bearing the title "The Boston College Inventory" under the same conditions and instructions as were used with the other groups. The second control group responded to an instrument which bore no title under modified instructions which are detailed in the section on Procedures.

Three null hypotheses were formulated for testing in this experiment; namely, there are no significant differences in mean scores on each of the four criterion scales:
1. between control group two (no threat or title) and the other seven groups considered together;
2. between control group one (neutral title) and the other six groups having titled inventories considered together; and
3. among experimental groups one through six.

PROCEDURES

Subjects

The population consisted of all first-year students enrolled in the Boston College School of Education, a total of 294. Each subject was assigned at random to one of the eight treatment groups, and rooms and proctors were assigned to the groups by lot. Since the tests were self-administering for all practical purposes, it was assumed that the particular proctor did not influence test-taking response set. Of the 294 requested, 265 students—186 females and 70 males—reported to the rooms assigned and completed the test.

Method

The items constituting the instrument were randomly ordered and mimeographed. A page of instructions was then prepared on which the test titles were overprinted. Thus, each test was identical to all others except that the title differed in each of the eight treatment groups. The instructions were adapted from those standard for the MMPI, changed only as required by the answer sheets used (Digitek Number DS 1120-A).

For the successful completion of the data-collection phase of the study, it was essential that no information regarding the study's nature reach the intended subjects prior to testing. Authorization to administer the tests was obtained from the associate dean for undergraduate studies, who was told simply that the writers wished to collect data on an experimental test. To insure the security of the instruments, the writers personally cut the stencils, mimeographed the tests, and assembled packages of tests, answer sheets and pencils, accomplishing this on a Sunday afternoon to avoid prying eyes. No one but the writers had any prior knowledge of the nature of the investigation.

Subjects were advised of their room assignments by posted notices three days prior to testing. No advanced notice of the purpose of the room assignments was given, and no questions were raised by the subjects, since such sessions were a routine part of the freshman orientation program in the School of Education.

Seven doctoral candidates who had previously served as proctors for the Boston College Office of Testing Services were requested to serve as proctors a few days in advance. They were told nothing of the study. A meeting of the proctors was held one hour prior to the time set for testing, and at this meeting the prepackaged test materials were distributed together with a brief sheet of instructions which were discussed. Even the investigators did not know which set of materials each proctor had, since only the packaged containing the untitled tests was identifiable.

From the preceding description it can be seen that all six experimental groups and the first control group were tested under very similar conditions. The second control group, intended to provide baseline data about how students would respond to the instrument under conditions of minimal threat, was handled differently. The Director of the Office of Testing Services served as proctor and explained to the subjects that it was the test items, and not themselves, that were being tested. Subjects were told not to enter their names or any identifying information on the answer sheets and were exhorted to respond candidly to each item in the interests of research. When all subjects had completed the test, they were asked to indicate their sex on the answer sheet, and all complied with this request. Subjects in the other groups recorded their names, student identification numbers and sex in order to simulate ordinary conditions of test administration. No time limit was imposed, and all subjects completed the test within 45 minutes.

Following the testing session, another meeting was held with the proctors to check for testing irregularites and explain the study. No irregularities were reported.

RESULTS

Means and standard deviations for each group on each variable are presented in Table 12-1.

Three planned contrasts (Hays, 1963, Chapter 14) were employed to test the three null hypotheses. The first of these compared mean

TABLE 12-1

Means and Standard Deviations for Each Group and Variable

Test Title (Group)	N	F-Scale Mean	S.D.	K-Scale Mean	S.D.	L-Scale Mean	S.D.	?-Score Mean	S.D.
Psych. Adj.	34	20.2	2.78	1.71	3.31	3.35	2.15	1.59	3.15
Acad. Pot.	32	20.7	2.96	17.5	3.84	4.00	1.97	1.09	2.08
Chris. Char.	37	19.9	3.30	17.0	3.22	3.16	1.72	1.70	3.56
Soc. Des.	35	20.8	3.42	16.8	3.48	3.91	2.02	1.91	3.67
Pol. Incl.	37	20.2	4.17	16.8	2.96	3.78	1.71	1.43	2.18
Att. Int.	26	19.7	2.77	17.2	2.95	4.31	1.92	1.73	2.80
B.C. Inv.	24	21.0	1.88	16.5	3.63	3.58	2.02	1.58	1.94
(No Title)	31	21.2	4.50	15.7	3.48	2.97	1.71	1.13	2.93

scores of subjects in control group one (no threat or title) with scores in all other groups considered together. Neither the F ratio for the F-scale variable nor that for the question (cannot decide) scale was significant at the .05 level. However, the F ratios for the K- and L-scale scores were each significant beyond the .05 level. Subjects in the no threat, no title control group had significantly lower scores on the K and L variables than all the other subjects combined.

The second null hypothesis was tested by comparing control group two (Boston College Inventory) with the other six groups having titled inventories. None of the F ratios for these four univariate analyses of variance was significant at the .05 level.

The third null hypothesis dealt with the possibility of mean differences among the six groups whose instruments bore "threat-producing" titles. Again, none of the four F ratios was significant at the .05 level.

DISCUSSION

Only the first of the three contrasts revealed significant differences. The baseline group (no threat, no title) scored lower than the other groups combined on both the K and L variables. To the extent that the K and L variables used in this experiment are comparable to K and L in the context of the full MMPI, it appears that subjects responding to titled tests responded to the items in the instrument more defensively and less honestly than did subjects who responded to the instrument which bore no title. But in that contrast, presence or absence of test title as a main effect was confounded with testing situation, as different directions were deliberately given to the baseline group.

More convincing evidence of the influence of test title alone as a main effect would have been produced if the second contrast had shown significant differences since in that situation testing conditions were virtually identical. No such differences were found, however. Moreover, the third contrast did not reveal any differences in pattern of response among the groups responding to instruments with different threat-producing titles.

It appears likely that the items in each form of the instrument were threatening in and of themselves by virtue of the nature of the information they requested. Thus, the hoped-for threat in titles may well have been defeated by the nature of the items. Response patterns to personality type tests may thus be more a function of the items such tests comprise than of their titles. Presumably, titles and items interact to contribute to response set. The particular set which develops could well vary not only for different types of item content, but for different types of individuals as well. These speculations will be the subject of further research.

References

Hathaway, S. R. & McKinley, J. C. *Minnesota Multiphasic Personality Inventory.* New York: The Psychological Corporation, 1943.

Hathaway, S. R. & McKinley, J. C. *Manual for the Minnesota Multiphasic Personality Inventory.* New York: The Psychological Corporation, 1951.

Hays, W. L. *Statistics for Psychologists.* New York: Holt, Rinehart and Winston, 1963.

Rothney, J. W., Danielson, P. J., & Heinmann, R. A. *Measurement for Guidance.* New York: Harper, 1959.

Authors

Jensen, John Anders *Address:* School of Ed., Boston Coll., Chestnut Hill, Mass. 02167. *Title:* Ass't Prof. *Degrees:* A.B. Cornell Univ., M.A., Ed.D., Univ. of Rochester. *Specializations:* Computer applications to education, statistics and measurement.

Schmitt, John A. *Address:* School of Ed., Boston Coll., Chestnut Hill, Mass. 02167. *Title:* Prof. *Degrees:* A.B. Villanova Coll., M.Ed., Ed.D., Cornell Univ. *Specializations:* Computer applications, systems analysis.

Questions on the Jensen and Schmitt aritcle.

1. Although the authors have stated that three null hypotheses were formulated, in reality several more individual null hypotheses were tested. Exactly how many were in fact tested?

VALIDITY AND PREDICTION STUDIES

2. List the null hypotheses that were rejected and the ones that were unable to be rejected.
3. Why did the authors test their null hypotheses by employing planned contrasts. What is the advantage of such a methodology over analysis of variance; over t tests?
4. In their discussion the authors report that the presence or absence of test title as a main effect was confounded with testing situation. How were they able to draw such a conclusion?
5. Of the four scales used by the authors which two appear to do the best job in supporting the first sentence of the last paragraph of the study?
6. If you were to suggest to the authors that a second table should be added to their study, exactly what would be reported in such a table?
7. Near the end of the research report the authors state that presumably, titles and items interact to contribute to response set. Have the authors tested for such an interaction? If not, how could it be tested?

SECTION III

CURRICULUM AND INSTRUCTION STUDIES

13

THE USE OF HIERARCHIES IN THE ANALYSIS AND PLANNING OF ALGEBRA INSTRUCTION

PETER W. AIRASIAN
Boston College
Boston, Massachusetts

With the advent of new curricula, materials, and approaches, algebra teachers are encountering a number of questions in the course of attempts to prepare their instruction. Teachers find themselves asking, how adequate is this chapter or learning unit? What are the specific strengths and weaknesses of this unit? How do the curriculum materials relate to my objectives? What changes should I make to facilitate my students' learning of this material? In order to answer these and the numerous other questions which can arise when lessons are planned in conjunction with new curriculum materials, teachers need some procedures which will enable them to obtain a clear picture of what is contained in a curriculum unit. They need this picture so that they can build their lessons around it, incorporating the adequate aspects of the materials and supplementing the inadequate aspects to bring them more in line with classroom objectives.

One approach to describing the contents of a curriculum unit has arisen from investigation of formative evaluation procedures (Airasian, 1968). In formative evaluation, an attempt is made to evaluate student performance on all objectives contained in a unit of curriculum material. In order to attain this goal, a means of specifying the objectives in curriculum units was devised. The method adopted involved the use of hierarchies of related objectives for describing and making decisions about the adequacy of curriculum units. The aim was to describe not only all the objectives contained in a unit, but also the extent to which objectives related to and built upon one another to produce an integrated unit. This article presents the results of a study which investigated the procedures developed for describing two algebra curriculum units in terms of hierarchies. In addition, samples of teacher comments based upon the described hierarchies are presented.

PROCEDURES

Two algebra teachers from different high schools were selected to describe hierarchies in two chapters of *Modern Algebra, Structure and*

Method, Book I (Dolciani et al, 1965). This text was selected because it was the classroom textbook used by the teachers. In order to insure that sufficient material was included to allow hierarchies to be manifested, a unit of learning was defined as a single chapter in the textbook.

The two algebra teachers were afforded practice in describing hierarchies. It was stressed that in each of the steps leading to the final description of a hierarchy, emphasis was to be centered solely upon the facets of the chapter being described. That is, the teachers were cautioned to describe only what was present in the chapters under study. Judgments about what content should have been included, at what behavior level the content should be taught, or what relationships might be introduced to tie material together were considered inappropriate for the initial stages of hierarchy description. An accurate description of a hierarchy was the desired end product of the procedures.

The first step in hierarchy description involved identifying the new content presented in the chapters. New content was defined as terms, facts, rules, skills, types of problems, etc. which had not been introduced to students in prior chapters of the textbook.

Having listed the new content, the teachers judged the behavior level at which each content was to be learned. This judgment was based upon the behavior level inferred from the textbook presentation. The question which the teachers were required to answer was, "At what behavior level does the textbook imply that this content element should be learned?" With slight modifications and additions, the *Taxonomy of Educational Objectives - Cognitive Domain,* (Bloom et al, 1956) served to define the behavior levels. The Taxonomy presents a series of behavior levels hierarchically organized according to complexity of behavior. The teachers were introduced to the Taxonomic categories and given practice in identifying behaviors at the different levels.

The last step in the description of the hierarchies involved positing relationships between content at different behavior levels. The teachers were required to judge which of the lower behavior level content elements were necessary but not sufficient prerequisites for learning the higher behavior level content elements. In general, this process involved inspecting the content at the highest behavioral level and asking what content, if any, at the next lowest behavioral level the textbook implied that the student must know in order to learn the highest level content. If no content in the next lower level was considered prerequisite, the third lowest level was inspected and the same question asked. This process was continued until a relationship between content at the highest level and content at some lower level was found, or until the lower level categories were exhausted. Having exhausted content at the highest level, the process was repeated for content at succeeding lower levels. Once the relationships for an entire chapter were specified by starting at the higher levels and working downwards, the process was repeated by starting with content at the lower behavioral levels and progressing upwards toward content at the higher behavioral levels. This second set of relationships served to check the accuracy of the first set of relationships.

The teachers were given about four weeks instruction and practice in describing the hierarchies of algebra units. At the end of this period, two successive chapters in the textbook were selected for study. The chapters were titled "Sentences in Two Variables" and "The Real Numbers." The two algebra teachers independently described the content, behaviors, and relationships in these chapters. The hierarchies described by the teachers were collected by the researcher for analysis.

RESULTS

Table 13-1 shows the agreement of the algebra teachers' description of the three facets of the hierarchies. The procedures instituted for hierarchy description did, after some training, permit the teachers to arrive independently at similar hierarchies for the chapters under study. Thus in algebra chapter number 1, the two teachers listed a combined total of 35 new content elements. Teacher 1 listed 15 of the content elements which teacher 2 listed, thereby producing agreement on 30 of the 35, or 85.7 percent, of the content listed in algebra chapter

TABLE 13-1

Agreement of Teachers on Content, Behavior Level, and Relationships for Hierarchies in Algebra

Subject Area	Chapter Number	Content Elements Identified Teacher 1	Content Elements Identified Teacher 2	Content Agreement Number	Content Agreement Per Cent	Per Cent Agreement Behavior Level	Relationships Identified Teacher 1	Relationships Identified Teacher 2	Relationship Agreement Number	Relationship Agreement Per Cent
Algebra	1	18	17	30	85.7	100.0	6	6	12	100.0
Algebra	2	43	39	74	90.2	97.7	16	19	32	91.5

1. The teachers agreed upon the implied behavior level for all of the 30 agreed upon content elements. This is equivalent to 100.0 percent agreement. Lastly, of the total of 12 relationships specified by both teachers, the teachers agreed upon all 12, or 100.0 percent.

In chapter 2 there was similar high agreement. The teachers agreed upon 90.2 percent of the new content contained in the chapter. The teachers classified the behavior levels of the agreed upon content with 97.7 percent agreement. Finally, of the 35 relationships specified by both teachers, there was agreement on 32, or 91.5 percent.

In general, there seemed to be only slight disagreement—less than 10 percent—between the teachers regarding behavioral classification and relationships. Given an element of content, the teachers could usually agree upon both the behavioral level at which it was to be learned and the other content elements to which it related. The teachers agreed less well upon the new content introduced in the chapters. However, this disagreement derived mainly from the inclusion or exclusion of new terms or facts by one or the other teacher. All content elements which the teachers failed to agree upon were inspected in the light of the final hierarchies. It became apparent that every disagreed upon element was an isolate relative to an entire chapter's hierarchy. That is, these content elements were not related to any other content elements. They were mainly terms and facts introduced once in the chapter and never used again after their introduction. Over all then, if the important content elements in the algebra chapters can be considered those which have relationships with other content elements, the procedures for hierarchy description produced high agreement between independent algebra teachers.

DISCUSSION

After describing the hierarchies for the algebra chapters, the teachers met with the researcher to discuss the implications of the hierarchies. From the standpoint of instruction, two facets of the hierarchies proved noteworthy. First the teachers commented upon the number of lower behavior level skills to be learned in a single textbook chapter. The large majority of new content in the chapters involved terms or facts which were learned principally through recall and remembering behaviors. Correspondingly, there seemed to be minor emphasis on such higher level behaviors as translation and application. The second noteworthy facet of the hierarchies commented upon by the teachers was the lack of relationships between the content elements. Even when a chapter possessed a number of relationships, as in algebra chapter 2, these elements did not build, one upon the other, to produce a single, integrated hierarchy. Rather, the hierarchies revealed three related

CURRICULUM AND INSTRUCTION STUDIES | 105

content elements here, and four there, each standing in isolation, rarely joining to produce a hierarchy leading to a single higher level content element. Even in a well-organized, logical subject area as algebra, the impression conveyed by the hierarchies was that students are presented with a plethora of terms and facts to be memorized, and that these terms and facts play a minor role in forming a basis for learning higher level behaviors.

Figure 13-1 shows the hierarchy described for the first algebra chapter. This hierarchy is representative of the hierarchy described for the second chapter. In the first algebra chapter, 15 new content elements were specified. Only four of these content elements were to be learned at a behavior level higher than recall. Only 6 relationships (indicated by connecting lines between content at the different behavior levels) were identified. Eight of the 15 content elements were isolates in the sense that they had no relationships with other content elements. Even when relationships were manifested, these did not build upon one another to integrate the entire chapter's objectives.

FIGURE 13-1

HIERARCHY FOR FIRST ALGEBRA CHAPTER

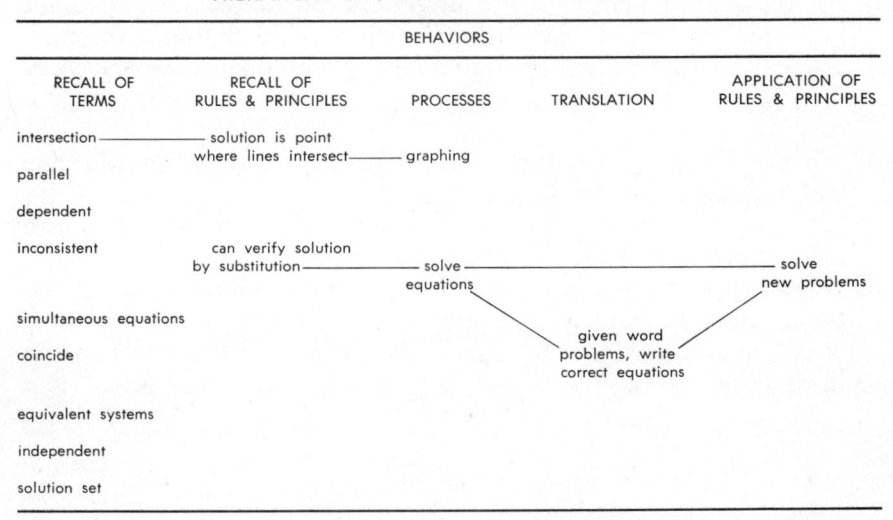

		BEHAVIORS		
RECALL OF TERMS	RECALL OF RULES & PRINCIPLES	PROCESSES	TRANSLATION	APPLICATION OF RULES & PRINCIPLES
intersection	solution is point where lines intersect	graphing		
parallel				
dependent				
inconsistent	can verify solution by substitution	solve equations		solve new problems
simultaneous equations			given word problems, write correct equations	
coincide				
equivalent systems				
independent				
solution set				

In the main, the chapters seemed to present a large number of unrelated content elements which were to be learned by memorization. Subjecting a chapter to a hierarchical analysis prior to planning instruction upon the chapter aided the teachers in determining where too much emphasis had been placed upon learning new terms or facts for their own sake or where relationships might be built into instruction to facilitate learning and transfer as the student progressed through higher and higher levels of behavioral complexity. At the very least, the hierarchical analysis revealed whether the chapters achieved all the teachers desired that they achieve. The use of hierarchical analysis in planning instruction or selecting curriculum materials could afford algebra teachers information regarding the contents of a curriculum unit. Hierarchies of related objectives can provide a map for planning instruction and supplementing curriculum materials to produce instruction compatible with teacher aims.

References

Airasian, Peter W. Formative Evaluation Instruments. *The Irish Journal of Education,* 1968, 2, 127-135.

Bloom, Benjamin S. et al. *Taxonomy of Educational Objectives, Handbook I: Cognitive Domain.* New York: David McKay Co., Inc., 1956.

Dolciani, Mary P., et al. *Modern Algebra, Structure and Method, Book I.* Boston: Houghton Mifflin Co., 1965.

Questions on the Airasian article.
1. What factors in the study hamper its generalizability to all high school algebra classes?
2. Although the teachers agreed in general on the content elements, behavior levels, and relationships in the algebra chapters, the study showed that there were areas of disagreement. How does one determine how much disagreement is too much disagreement in studies such as this one?
3. What would have been the advantage of having three teachers analyze the algebra chapters?
4. What were the advantages of selecting material familiar to the teachers for analysis? What were the disadvantages?
5. Often, the data for research are based upon the judgements of "experts." Such judgements are open to many forms of bias. List some of these sources of bias and describe how this study tried to overcome these biases.

14

A RELATIONSHIP BETWEEN TELEVISION WATCHING AND ACADEMIC ACHIEVEMENT IN ENGLISH

PRISCILLA WETMORE
Dracut Public Schools
Dracut, Massachusetts

ABSTRACT

This study was undertaken to determine whether or not the number of hours a child spends watching television is related to his grade point average (GPA) in English. The study applied to advanced placement and average placement eighth grade students at Dracut Junior High School, Dracut, Massachusetts.

A television questionnaire was administered to all advanced placement students (85) and to all average placement students (89). A random sample of both groups was taken. Two Pearson Product Moment correlation coefficients were computed. Both comparisons, one between hours of television viewing and GPA in English of advanced students, and one between hours of television viewing and GPA in English of average students, showed significantly high negative relationships.

These results suggest that if a child spends a considerable amount of time per week watching television, his grades in English will be inversely proportional to that time.

INTRODUCTION

Most parents are concerned with their children's achievement in school and are quite interested in factors that may affect it. They realize that a multitude of factors affect a student's achievement in school. This study is based on the researcher's assumption that the number of hours a child spends watching television has an inverse relation to achievement. In other words, the more a child watches television, the less he will achieve in school.

A recent article in *TV Guide* has this to say about younger children and TV watching.

In early grade school, brighter children tend to do more TV watching. But by the time the intelligent child is in the 10-13 age bracket, a major shift in habit occurs; he departs the ranks of heavy viewers ... (Hickey, 1969b p. 8).

As far as achievement is concerned, *TV Guide* refers only to vocabulary:

In the early grades, it has been shown that vocabulary is greatly enhanced by much TV viewing. It seems clear that, to a child, exposure to several hundred words is of great educational value. (Effrom, 1969 p. 7.)

This area of vocabulary seems to be the only one in which actual tests have been conducted to determine the effects of TV watching on education.

The articles also seem to indicate that the brighter children, after the age of ten, become bored with TV because it no longer offers any challenge to their intellects.

Why do some children, even bright children, continue watching TV even when it offers no challenge?

A child who watches 'too much' television usually is suffering some emotional distress which is causing him to retreat into TV watching. (Hickey, 1969a p. 6.)

Hickey's recommendation to parents is as follows:

In homes where a parent reads to the child and is reasonably attentive to his natural curiosity and desire for actual experience rather than vicarious experience, the child automatically watches television less. (Hickey, 1969a p. 7.)

There are opposing views as to how healthy an educational force TV is. Some say it is educationally profitable, while others say it is detrimental. However, all seem to agree that generally speaking the worst students are heavy viewers. It was the purpose of this study to determine the relationship between classroom achievement and hours of television viewing for both *average* placement and *advanced* placement students. Since it would be difficult to provide a measure of actual classroom achievement that would cover all subjects, achievement was limited to the subject of English. Also, only eighth grade students were used in the study sample.

HYPOTHESES

For this study the following research hypotheses were drawn:
1. The number of hours of television viewing is inversely related to GPA in English of advanced eighth grade students.
2. The number of hours of television viewing is inversely related to GPA in English of average eighth grade students.

The null hypotheses tested in this study were as follows:
1. The number of hours of television viewing is not inversely related to GPA in English of advanced eighth grade students.
2. The number of hours of television viewing is not inversely related to GPA in English of average eighth grade students.

SAMPLE

As shown in Table 14-1, in the Dracut Junior High School there are a total of 88 advanced placement students divided into three groups of equal ability. Students are categorized as advanced placement students by a variety of factors, including a minimum Otis Beta IQ of 120, previous achievement, and teachers' recommendations. Due to absences only 85 of these 88 students were administered the questionnaire. A random sample of 43 was selected for this study by accepting every other questionnaire.

From a total of 100 average placement students divided into four groups of equal ability 89 were present the day that the questionnaire was administered. With the exception of the IQ criterion the factors for placing students into the average placement classes were similar to those for placing students into advanced placement classes. Average placement students obtain Otis Beta IQ scores of between 85-100. A random sample of 45 students was selected for this study in a manner similar to that for the advanced sample.

TABLE 14-1

Actual Number of Students in Each Group

Group	Advanced N	Average N
1	30	25
2	30	25
3	28	25
4	0	25
Total	88	100

INSTRUMENTATION

For each of the groups, advanced and average, the researcher used the first quarter report card marks of the students to determine the

GPA for English achievement. To determine the amount of television viewing that was done by each child, a questionnaire was administered. This questionnaire contained a number of questions (see Appendix), but only the answers to question number 7 were considered. The other questions were devised so that the true purpose of the questionnaire would be disguised. This would allow for more accurate, undeliberate responses. These other items could also be used for a data pool for additional research.

DESIGN

The answers to item 7 in the questionnaire were summed so that a weekly total of hours of television viewing could be obtained. These totals were then graphed with English grades to see if there were a linear relationship. Since a linear relationship did exist, the Pearson Product Moment correlation coefficient was computed. Because there was such a difference in the two sets of data (the TV hours ranging from 4 to 56, and the GPA ranging from 50 to 95) both were converted to standard T scores. In order to determine whether or not there was any relationship between hours of television viewing and GPA in English, two Pearson Product Moment correlation coefficients were computed, one for the advanced group and one for the average group. The results are reported in Tables 14-2 and 14-3.

TABLE 14-2

Correlation between Number of Hours of TV Viewing and GPA in English of Advanced Students

	TV Hours	GPA
N	43	43
Mean (standard score)	50.1	50.0
SD (standard score)	9.8	10.2
r (Pearson-Product)	—.72*	

*Significant at the .01 level.

RESULTS

Tables 14-2 and 14-3 clearly indicate that the relationships for both groups are indeed significant. In fact, both are significant beyond the

TABLE 14-3

Correlation between Number of Hours of TV Viewing and GPA in English of Average Students

	TV Hours	GPA
N	45	45
Mean (standard score)	50.6	51.2
SD (standard score)	10.1	10.0
r (Pearson-Product)	—.55*	

*Significant at the .01 level.

.01 level of probability. The negative coefficients indicate inverse relationships. That means that the higher the number of hours of television viewing, the lower the GPA in English and vice versa. Since both coefficients are significant, and the null hypotheses of no inverse relationships are rejected, one can be 99% confident that each inverse correlation coefficient could not happen by chance. It is interesting to note that the coefficient for the advanced group (–.72) is substantially higher than that for the average group (–.55). This indicates that the relationship holds true for both groups, but more so for the advanced groups. Since the amount of explained variance between the two variables is shown by r^2, it can be seen that 52% of the variance between the advanced placement GPA and TV viewing is explained whereas only 30% is explained for the average placement students.

LIMITATIONS

This particular study was limited to eighth grade students in the Dracut Junior High School. Therefore, the results can not be interpreted to refer to any other group.

Another limitation of the study is the fact that several teachers were involved in the marking of the students in English. Each teacher had his own criterion for marking, and comparability of scoring criteria was certainly not established.

Also the GPA in English represents only a quarter mark. A better indication of GPA would be to take final grades in June which are a summation and average of the quarter marks. However, time did not allow this.

IMPLICATIONS

For further research it is suggested that a wider geographical and chronological sampling of students be obtained. The results would have a much broader interpretation. It would be interesting to see if the same results would occur with younger or older students, or with students from different parts of the country. Also, a suggestion for further research would be to check the relationship between TV viewing and GPA in subjects other than English. However, to achieve more accurate results for any of these suggested studies, a more standard and representative method of marking students would be required.

A high correlation does not indicate a cause and effect relationship. In *TV Guide,* an implication is made that a child who watches too much TV and is bored with it has an emotional problem. A need for further investigation of this fact would seem apparent. Perhaps these emotional problems developed because the child has always been a poor achiever, particularly in reading.

Present literature further implies that parents must set an "example" as far as television viewing is concerned. They need to interest their children in other forms of amusement and entertainment. It would seem that if parents could accomplish this, children would do less TV watching.

SUMMARY

For advanced and average eighth grade students in the Dracut Junior High School, television viewing has a significant and inverse relationship with GPA in English. Although this is true for all eighth grade students, it is more indicative of the advanced placement groups than of the average groups.

References

Effrom, E. "Television as a Teacher." *TV Guide.* October 25, 1969, 17, 7.
Hickey, N. "Our Greatest Natural Resourse: Our Children." *TV Guide.* November 29, 1969, 17, 6.
Hickey, N. "What is TV Doing to Them?" *TV Guide.* October 11, 1969, 17.

APPENDIX

Name _____
Grade _____
Age _____
years   mos.

Television Questionnaire
1. What's your favorite television program? _____
2. Do you have a color television set in your home? _____

3. How many television sets are there in your home? 1 2 3 4
4. Do you watch television alone or with other people? _____
5. Circle the latest time you stay up watching television. 9:00 -9:30
   -10:00 -10:30 -11:00 -11:30 12:00 -12:30 -1:00
6. Which is your favorite night to watch television? Circle one. Sunday, Monday, Tuesday, Wednesday, Thursday, Friday, Saturday
7. Circle the number of hours you watch television on the follwing nights:

Sunday	0	1/2	1	1 1/2	2	2 1/2	3	3 1/2	4	4 1/2	5	5 1/2	6	6 1/2	7	7 1/2	8
Monday	0	1/2	1	1 1/2	2	2 1/2	3	3 1/2	4	4 1/2	5	5 1/2	6	6 1/2	7	7 1/2	8
Tuesday	0	1/2	1	1 1/2	2	2 1/2	3	3 1/2	4	4 1/2	5	5 1/2	6	6 1/2	7	7 1/2	8
Wednesday	0	1/2	1	1 1/2	2	2 1/2	3	3 1/2	4	4 1/2	5	5 1/2	6	6 1/2	7	7 1/2	8
Thursday	0	1/2	1	1 1/2	2	2 1/2	3	3 1/2	4	4 1/2	5	5 1/2	6	6 1/2	7	7 1/2	8
Friday	0	1/2	1	1 1/2	2	2 1/2	3	3 1/2	4	4 1/2	5	5 1/2	6	6 1/2	7	7 1/2	8
Saturday	0	1/2	1	1 1/2	2	2 1/2	3	3 1/2	4	4 1/2	5	5 1/2	6	6 1/2	7	7 1/2	8

8. Check the types of programs you watch from the following list:
   ____ documentaries
   ____ comedies
   ____ movies
   ____ serials
   ____ educational programs
   ____ varieties
   ____ cartoons
   ____ sports

Questions for the Wetmore article.
1. Discuss the acceptability of the author's random sampling technique. How would you have sampled?
2. Was it necessary for the author to convert his raw scores to standard scores? If she did not convert the raw scores, would her correlation results have changed? If so, in what way?
3. The author has indicated several "limitations" of her study. What other limitations does the study have which she failed to mention?
4. Exactly what does the author mean when she states that 52% of the variance between GPA and TV viewing is explained?
5. The author points out that, "a high correlation does not indicate a cause and effect relationship." How would one go about proving that TV viewing does or does not cause low GPA?
6. In the questionnaire given to the student, information on many other variables was collected but not used by the author. Briefly design a study which would make use of one or more of these other variables.

15

THE EFFECTS OF ALTERNATIONS BETWEEN CONDITIONS OF QUIET AND MUSIC UPON READING SPEED AND COMPREHENSION

BERNARD M. REARDON
Peabody Public Schools
Peabody, Massachusetts

ABSTRACT

The reading speed and comprehension of 20 female juniors at Merrimack College were tested through a series of 13 exercises, four of which were completed under conditions of quiet, six under conditions of music and three once again in a quiet situation. There was a significant difference among all transitional exercises for mean completion times (CMPTLs). There was a significant decrease in mean comprehension scores (CMPs) in the transitional exercises and this significance was specifically found between the last exercise of the first quiet periods (FQP) and the first exercise of the first music period (FMP). This could show an inability for instant adjustment by Ss; but the CMPs increased and CMPLTs decreased with successive exercises which possibly indicate an adjustive ability.

INTRODUCTION

Problems relating to the influence of distracting stimuli upon "mental work" and upon attentive attitudes involved in the performance of tasks have long held the interest of experimental psychologists. One of the first thorough investigations of this subject was performed by J. J. B. Morgan in 1916 (Crafts, Schenirla, Robinson, and Gilbert, 1950, pp. 233-234). Having required each subject (S) to perform a series of complicated decoding tasks alternately in periods of quiet and noise, Morgan found that "noise causes an initial slowing in speed followed by an increase, while the removal of noises causes a retardation followed by normal" (Morgan, 1916). Furthermore, although there appeared no consistent increase in errors of performance during the noisy periods, measurements of pressure and breathing activities indicated that the S put forth extra effort in order to overcome the effects of distraction (Crafts, Scheirla, Robinson, and Gilbert, 1950, p. 235).

In an experiment similar to Morgan's, Ford, (1929), attempted to ascertain the effects of the introduction and removal of distracting auditory stimuli upon the efficiency of performance from problem to problem in a series. Employing a series of tasks in which the S was to note, add, and record all of the numbers in a row of mixed letters and numerals using an automobile horn as a distracting mechanism, Ford discovered that the beginnings of both the noise and quiet periods were marked by a definite lengthening of solution time and that this effect was more pronounced for the noise period. As in the case of Morgan, it was found that although the auditory stimulation had little, if any, effect on the accuracy of the S's performance, the S did expend greater effort while the noise persisted. Notwithstanding his more sophisticated explanation of the physiological changes during auditory stimulation, Freeman, in 1939, reached the same conclusion as did Morgan and Ford with reference to the S's apparent ability to adapt to a change in environmental conditions during the performance of a series of tasks (Crafts, Scheiria, Robinson, and Gilbert, 1950, p. 242).

Concerning himself with a more practical aspect of the problem, Fendrick, (1937), determined to measure the difference in reading efficiency that might manifest itself when college students were asked to study a selected assignment in the classroom with and without distraction by phonograph music. Using the equivalent group method of experimentation, Fendrick found that: (1) the control group scored higher on a test of their comprehension than did the distracted group; (2) there was a gradual increase in the size of the differences between the average scores for distracted and non-distracted Ss as their quintile level of intelligence became higher; and (3) the distracted Ss read a greater amount of material in the alloted time.

Subsequent to Fredrick's experiment, a majority of the investigators in this general field have turned their attention to the relative effects of different types of music upon reading efficiency and verbal learning (Henderson, Crews, and Barlow, 1945; Freeburne, and Fleischer, 1952). Contrary to the conclusion of Fendrick, Freeburne and Fleischer (1925), Hall (1952) reported a facilitating effect of background music upon reading comprehension for students of below average intelligence and achievement.

PURPOSE

The purpose of this study was to determine whether or not the adaptation process, noted by Morgan, Ford, and Freeman, is operative for individuals in the "reading-with-music" situation.

The null hypotheses are: (1) that there will be no difference among mean CMPLTs for transitional exercises; and (2) that there will be no difference among mean CMPs for transitional exercises. CMPLTs refers to the mean completion times in seconds. CMPs refer to the mean raw comprehension scores.

METHOD

Materials and Apparatus

The apparatus used consisted of: (1) room with a desk; (2) stop clock; (3) General Electric portable stereo (concealed from sight set at same volume for each S; (4) "Rhapsody in Blue" (33-1/3 rpm) by George Gershwin as interpreted by the Philadelphia Orchestra under the direction of Eugene Ormandy (Columbia recording, ML 4026); (5) Thirteen 450-word reading exercises with accompanying ten questions, two option multiple-choice comprehension tests. The 13 exercises presented in this study were designed for a second-year college proficiency level by Science Research Associates, Inc.

Experimental Design

The absence or presence of music constituted the independent variable whose effects were measured upon the dependent variable, the reading speed and comprehension of the Ss. Control over the effects of the time of testing upon performance was achieved by testing all Ss between the hours of 7 p.m. and 10 p.m. on successive evenings. To eliminate the goal gradient effect, the number of exercises in the first and fourth periods of testing was varied. In accordance with this same purpose, separate answer sheets were provided for each exercise. While the variable factor of fatigue was treated by allowing the Ss a three minute rest between the testing periods, the possible effects of this interval upon performance were investigated by interposing a rest period within the condition of musical stimulation. A semi-classical music selection was chosen in order to obtain a balance between the high association value that would probably exist with popular music and the relatively non-distracting nature of classical music established by previous experiments (Henderson, Crews, and Barlow, 1945).

Uncontrolled variables included each S's degree of motivation and concentration upon the task, his intelligence and reading achievement level, his study habits, and his interest in the subject matter of the reading selections employed.

Procedure

The Ss were tested individually by the experimenter (E) under equivalent conditions in an experimental room. Testing was performed every evening between the hours of 7 p.m. and 10 p.m. over a period of successive days. Each S was required to read 13 equally difficult selections of approximately 450 words each and to answer 10 multiple-choice questions pertaining to the contents of each selection.

Seated at the desk in a position which did not afford a view of the phonograph, the S was initially presented with a group of four exercises, each of which he was to complete in turn under quiet conditions while being timed by the E. (first quiet period = FQP). Following a rest period of three minutes, E introduced the music of Gershwin's "Rhapsody in Blue" into the experimental situation and presented S with a series of three exercises for each of which the completion time was recorded. (first music period = FMP). The music persisted throughout the three minute rest interval subsequent to the second test period. The third test period involving three selections, (second music period = SMP), was followed by a three minute musical rest period. The music was discontinued as S began the fourth test period, consisting of three individually timed exercises (second quiet period = SQP).

Prior to the beginning of the experiment, E read the following instructions to S: "You will be given several groups of exercises; each exercise will consist of a short reading selection followed by 10 multiple-choice questions. You are to read each selection at the most rapid rate to which you are accustomed. You are to answer all of the questions as best you can on the basis of the information you have obtained from the reading material. Once again you are asked to work as rapidly and as accurately as possible. Do not look back to the selection while answering the question; neither are you to look at the questions before you begin reading. Mark the letter of your choice on the answer sheet with which you will be provided. Permit no interference from anything while you are working. You will be informed when you have completed a group of exercises and will be given a three minute rest period between groups. You are to begin reading each exercise when I say 'Ready ... Go!!! and you are to indicate when you have finished the questions by placing your pencil down on the table. Are there any questions? Ready ... Go!

Subjects

Ss were 20 randomly selected 19 and 20 year old female juniors at Merrimack College, North Andover, Massachusetts.

Data Analysis

Each subject was administered 13 exercises. The results of the first exercise of the FQP were discarded, since they were used as a warm-up exercise for the subjects. Thus, the measurements considered were the remaining three exercises of the first quiet period (FQP), the six during musical stimulation (FMP and SMP), and the three during the SQP.

118 | CURRICULUM AND INSTRUCTION STUDIES

Mean CMPLTs (completion time in seconds) and mean CMPs (score = number right minus number wrong) for all Ss were computed separately for each exercise. Mean CMPLTs and CMPs were plotted as functions of the positions of an exercise in the series. An analysis of variance was applied for the three transitional exercises taken together for both mean CMPLTs and mean CMPs. Transitional exercises are those two that involve changes of conditions (quiet to music, exercises 3 and 4, T_1, and music to quiet exercises 9 and 10, T_3, and a control period of no change of condition, music to music, exercises 6 and 7, T_2). t-tests for the difference between correlated means for the transitional exercises of mean CMPs and mean CMPLTs taken separately were applied when the analysis of variances of combined transitional exercises of CMPs and CMPLTs proved to be significant. The t-tests were used to determine exactly which transitions were significantly different.

TABLE 15-1

Mean Completion Times, Comprehension Scores, and Transition Point Differences for Successively Performed Exercises

Exercise	Mean Completion Time (secs.)	Difference between Transitional Exercises (secs.)	Mean Comprehension Score (Score = Number right—Number wrong)	Difference between Transitional Exercises (secs.)
1	247.1		+2.4	
2	203.5		+4.3	
3	219.2		+6.3	
		$T_1 = 19$		$T_1 = 8.6$
4	238.2		−2.3	
5	236.6		+2.8	
6	220.8		+5.0	
		$T_2 = 17.6$		$T_2 = .5$
7	238.4		+5.5	
8	223.0		+5.4	
9	211.4		+5.6	
		$T_3 = 44.9$		$T_3 = .4$
10	256.3		+5.2	
11	260.7		−1.0	
12	249.6		+2.8	

RESULTS

Table 15-1 summarizes the mean CMPLTs and mean CMPs for each exercise. The important transitional exercises show differences in means in both mean CMPLTs and mean CMPs. Regarding mean CMPLTs, the results show the difference of T_1 as increasing 19 secs., T_2 shows an increase of 17.6 secs., and T_3 shows an increase of 44.9 secs., as the condition changed from music to quiet. Regarding mean CMPs, the results show T_1 decreasing 8.6, T_2 increasing .5 and T_3 decreasing .4.

Table 15-2 presents the results of the analysis of variance performed on the mean combined CMPLTs for transitional exercises. The F ratio was significant beyond the .05 probability level. The F required at the

TABLE 15-2

Analysis of Variance: Mean Completion Times for Transitional Exercise Taken Together

Source of Variation	Degrees of Freedom	Sum of Squares	Mean Squares	F
Between Groups	5	29727.4	5959.58	
Within Groups	114	257975.67	2262.94	
Total	119	287723.07		2.68*

*Significant at .05 level.

TABLE 15-3

Analysis of Variance: Mean Comprehension Score for Combined Transitional Exercises Taken Together

Source of Variation	Degrees of Freedom	Sum of Squares	Mean Squares	F
Between Groups	5	1029.6	205.92	
Within Groups	114	1093.0	9.59	
Total	119	2122.6		21.47*

*Significant at the .01 level.

.05 level for significance was 2.29 and the computed F of 2.68 exceeds this figure.

Table 15-3 presents the results of the analysis of variance performed on the mean combined CMPs for transitional exercises. The F ratio was significant at the .01 level. The F required at the .01 level for significance is 3.17 and the computed F of 21.47 far exceeds the required F.

TABLE 15-4

Results of t-Tests Performed on Mean Completion Times of Successive Transitional Exercises

	\multicolumn{6}{c}{Transitional Exercises}
	T_1		T_2		T_3	
Components	#3(Q)	#4(M)	#6(M)	#7(M)	#9(M)	#10(Q)
N	20	20	20	20	20	20
$\overline{X}$	220.0	238.2	220.9	230.3	206.5	256.0
SD	31.17	30.98	38.8	30.02	32.9	31.9
t	−4.8*		−2.37**		−12.82*	

*Significant at .01 level.
**Significant at .05 level.

Table 15-4 presents the results of the *t*-tests performed on the mean CMPLTs for successive transitional exercises. The combined CMPLTs showed significance. Thus in order to examine the nature of the difference, the *t*-tests for means of correlated data were completed. Each component of the transitional exercises was taken separately, T_1 (exercises 3 and 4), T_2 (exercises 6 and 7), and T_3 (exercises 9 and 10). The results show a *t* ratio of −4.8 between T_1 means and a *t* ratio of −12.82 between T_3 means. Both these computed *t* ratios far exceed the required *t* for significance of 2.423 at the .01 level. The *t* ratio of −2.37 represented between the T_2 means is significant at the .05 level (required *t* of 1.684).

Table 15-5 demonstrates the results of the *t*-tests performed on the mean CMPs for successive, transitional exercises. T_2 and T_3 resulted in *t* ratios in −.49 and .32 respectively. Both these results fall far short of 1.684 required for signifcance at the .05 level. T_1 had a *t* of 6.04 which far exceed the *t* of 2.423 required for significance at the .01 level.

Summarizing the results, the two analyses of variance each proved significant. Mean CMPLTs were found significant at .05 level for T_2 and at the .01 level for T_1 and T_3. Mean CMPs were found to be significant only at T_1 and T_3. Mean CMPs were found to be significant at T_1 (at the .01 level).

TABLE 15-5

Results of t-Tests Performed on Mean Comprehension Scores of Successive Transitional Exercises

	\multicolumn{6}{c}{Transitional Exercises}
	\multicolumn{2}{c}{T_1}	\multicolumn{2}{c}{T_2}	\multicolumn{2}{c}{T_3}
Components	#3(Q)	#4(M)	#6(M)	#7(M)	#9(M)	#10(Q)
N	20	20	20	20	20	20
$\bar{X}$	6.3	−2.35	5.05	5.5	5.65	5.25
SD	3.23	5.74	1.99	1.65	2.57	4.45
t		6.04*		−.49**		.32*

*Significant at .01 level.
**Not significant at .05 level.

DISCUSSION

The first null hypothesis of no difference among mean CMPLTs for transitional exercises was able to be rejected at the .05 probability level. That is, the differences in the results obtained concerning mean CMPLTs can be attributed to chance only five times in a hundred. Additional *t*-tests on the successive transitional exercises taken in pairs shows that the increase of 44.9 seconds over T_3 (i.e. 9 and 10) was significant at the .01 level. Thus, only one in one hundred times would the same results be expected due to chance. T_1 (19 secs.) and T_2 (17.6 secs.) also showed increases and these increases were significant at the .05 probability level.

The analysis of variance among mean CMPs for transitional exercises allows us to reject the second null hypothesis at the .01 probability level. Additional *t*-tests to determine where the significance lies in the transitional exercises indicated that only T_1 showed any significant difference (P<.01). T_2 and T_3 had no significant difference as was theorized since the actual differences were only chance ones.

A visual analysis of the trends of each exercise (Ex) might be helpful since only the transitional exercises were considered in the statistical analyses. The decrease between Ex 1 and Ex 2 might be significant.

Then it seems as if an adaptive process takes place until finally T_1 shows an increase. In FMP the S might have adapted only to be thrown off perhaps by the rest period. Again the S betters his score in SMP; in T_3 there is a big increase; this is followed by a leveling off in SQP. For CMPLTs, perhaps the rest period had a negative effect on the Ss.

For CMPs and Ss seem to show an increased scoring through FQP and a big decrease in T_1. In FMP and SMP the S again adapt to the music as demonstrated by the increasing or relatively stable CMPs. In SQP the S may have become fatigued or bored. In fact, any number of factors could have caused the sudden drop between Ex 10 and 11.

It seems that CMPLTs were more affected in the transitional exercises than CMPs. However, the transitional exercises were designed to determine whether the change of condition (both ways) or no change had any effect on CMPLTs. It may have occurred that a negative effect of the rest periods has resulted. Perhaps a future study might eliminate rest periods. As far as CMPs is concerned, only the initial transitional exercise showed any difference worth noting. It seems, then, that the girls comprising the sample were affected by the changing condition (or rest period) each time in CMPLTs but were only affected at the initial condition change for CMPs. This leads to the belief that perhaps music only superficially affects reading ability (CMPLTs), but does not in fact, affect comprehension for these Ss. These Ss were able to adapt to the condition changes and therefore maintain a relative constancy of comprehension.

After each experiment, each S was questioned and each specifically stated that she did not study with music. Perhaps these Ss would be able to use music in their studying and after adaptation might even improve the results of study. Future experiments might disregard the rest periods, start with music, or score the CMPs differently. This experiment did not consider fatigue, interest of each S in the articles, past backgrounds or any other such information. Perhaps future studies might be able to devise a design to study these factors.

SUMMARY

This study was interested in reading rate (CMPLT) and in reading comprehension (CMP) under varying conditions of music and quiet. The transitional exercises between conditions of music and quiet were of specific importance. With regard to reading speed, an overall slowing down resulted no matter what condition existed. A change from quiet to music or music to quiet or no change at all resulted in a slowing down over the previous time. With regard to comprehension, only the initial change from quiet to music seemed to have had a significant effect on reading comprehension. An adaptation seems to have occurred.

The results seem to point to further studies in the areas of conditions necessary for complete concentration. It seems possible that slight background noise might be overcome by appropriate musical arrangements in such a way as to increase reading comprehension, and even reading speed. Supervised courses in study habits for high school students might utilize such techniques, while individualizing these techniques where needed.

References

Crafts, L. W., Schneirla, T. C., Robinson, E. E., and Gilbert, R. W., *Recent experiments in psychology.* New York: McGraw-Hill, 1950.

Fredrick, P. The influence of musical distraction upon reading efficiency. *Journal of Educational Research,* 1937, 3, 264-271.

Ford, A. Attention-automatization: an investigation of the transitional nature of mind. *American Journal of Psychology,* 1929, 41, 1-32.

Freeburne, C. M., and Fleischer, M. The effect of music distraction upon reading rate and comprehension. *Journal of Educational Psychology,* 1952, 43, 101-109.

Hall, J. C. The effect of background music on the reading comprehension of twenty-eight eighth and ninth grade students. *Journal of Educational Research,* 1952, 45, 451-458.

Henderson, M. T., Crews, A., and Barlow, J. A study of the effect of music distraction on reading efficiency. *Journal of Applied Psychology,* 1945, 29, 313-317.

Questions on the Reardon article.
1. In Table 15-2, assume that the degrees of freedom and the sums of squares are correct. Check the accuracy of the mean squares and the F ratio reported.
2. What are the assumptions of analysis of variance? Do you think that the author has met these assumptions? How could one test the assumption of homogenity of variance?
3. What argument could be given for the inadvisability of performing a series of t tests after one has determined a significant analysis of variance F ratio?
4. In Table 15-4 negative t ratios are reported. How does the interpretation of a negative t ratio differ from the interpretation of a positive t ratio? Is it possible to obtain a negative F ratio and/or a negative chi square?
5. The author admits that this study did not control for the fatigue factor. Is this a legitimate limitation of the study? If so, could you suggest a way to control for such a factor?

16

A COMPARISON OF A TRANSFORMATIONAL LINGUISTICS PROGRAM WITH A MORE TRADITIONAL LINGUISTICS PROGRAM IN GRADES FIVE AND SIX

RICHARD BROWNELL and JOHN P. McMATH
Danvers Public Schools
Danvers, Massachusetts

INTRODUCTION

The purpose of this study was to determine the effects that a transformational Linguistics English program had on fifth and sixth-grade students classified as brighter students in comparison to the effects of a more traditional linguistics approach which was conducted for fifth and sixth-grade children considered generally of lesser ability. This study attempted to determine the extent to which each fifth-grade group was able to improve in verb recognition and usage. The study also attempted to determine the extent to which each sixth-grade group was able to improve in the recognition of adverbs and adverbials.

METHODOLOGY

Thirty sixth-grade students and 43 fifth-grade students of the Danvers Public Schools, Danvers, Massachusetts, were the subjects of this research. The sixth-grade students consisted of two groups. The first group of 13 students was the brighter group (Otis Beta Mean I.Q. of 118). The second group of 17 students was of average intelligence (Otis Beta Mean I.Q. of 103). The brighter group was challenged with a transformational approach to English Grammar (Roberts), a system with which they were totally unfamiliar. The average group of 17 sixth-grade students was exposed to a similar unit of grammar utilizing the more familiar and traditional linguistic (Laidlaw) approach. Each group was pre-tested with a teacher-made 50 item test purporting to cover the objectives of the three week unit on adverbs and adverbials. The content validity of the tests was determined by a team of teachers familiar with both the Laidlaw and Roberts approaches. Special care was taken to assure that the two tests were comparable in terms of average item difficulty. A three week instructional period was given to each group by the same teacher covering the common, operational and agreed upon objectives which were the basis of the pre-tests. At the end of the instructional period each student was administered the test he had taken before the instructional period.

During the same period of time, 43 fifth-grade students were the subjects of a similar study. Like the sixth-grade students, they were divided into two groups of varying intellectual potential. The brighter of the two groups (Otis Beta Mean I.Q. of 120) was taught a specific unit of grammar utilizing the Roberts Linguistics approach while the other group (Otis Beta Mean I.Q. of 106) was taught a similar unit utilizing the Laidlaw approach. Similar pre-testing, instructional and post-testing procedures were conducted on these groups in a manner described previously for the sixth-grade groups. The objectives covered were in the area of verb recognition and usage.

DESIGN AND HYPOTHESES

Specifically, on the basis of pre- and post-tests scores on both Roberts and Laidlaw units of work, this study tested the following null hypotheses:

1 H_o: There is no significant difference between the pre- and post-test mean scores of fifth-grade students studying the usage of principal parts of verbs from the Laidlaw Series.

2 H_o: There is no significant difference between the pre- and post-test mean scores of fifth-grade students studying the usage of principal parts of verbs from the Roberts Series.

3 H_o: There is no significant difference between the pre- and post-test mean scores of sixth-grade students studying the recognition of adverbs and adverbials from the Laidlaw Series.

4 H_o: There is no significant difference between the pre- and post-test mean scores of sixth-grade students studying the recognition of adverbs and adverbials from the Roberts Series.

5 H_o: There is no significant difference between the rates of growth of fifth-grade pupils using Laidlaw when individual scores are adjusted for intelligence.

6 H_o: There is no significant difference between the rates of growth of sixth-grade pupils using Roberts and sixth-grade pupils using Laidlaw when individual scores are adjusted for intelligence.

The statistical model chosen to test null hypotheses 1-4 was the t test. The results are reported in Tables 16-1 and 16-2.

The model chosen to test null hypotheses 5 and 6 was the analysis of covariance. The results are reported in Tables 16-3 and 16-4.

LIMITATIONS

The samples used for the study were purposive in nature and in no way represented a larger defined population. Thus conclusions drawn in this study are statistically valid only for the samples used.

That part of the experiment dealing with pupils of grade six was conducted in the same classroom where both groups were housed. As a result, both groups could not avoid being "exposed" to a certain amount of the other group's instruction.

No prediction can be made as to what would happen if the Roberts students had been exposed to Roberts Linguistics over a significant number of years.

Although the team of teachers took great care to assure comparability of item difficulty between the Laidlaw and Roberts tests, item difficulties were not determined empirically.

RESULTS

The data in Table 16-1 show that null hypotheses 1 and 2 were both rejected at the .01 probability level. It can be concluded that both the fifth-grade Roberts students and the fifth-grade Laidlaw students improved significantly in the usage of principal parts of verbs, and that such a difference could appear by chance alone less than one time in 100.

TABLE 16-1

Means, Standard Deviations and t Ratios for 5th Grade Pre- and Post-Test Scores of Roberts and Laidlaw Students

	Roberts Pretest	Roberts Post-test	Laidlaw Pretest	Laidlaw Post-test
N	22	22	21	21
X	20.09	39.86	33.04	39.00
SD	10.84	8.45	3.77	4.90
t	6.59*		3.84*	

*$p < .01$

Similarly, the data in Table 16-2 show that null hypotheses 3 and 4 were both rejected at the .01 probability level. It can be concluded that

CURRICULUM AND INSTRUCTION STUDIES | 127

both the sixth-grade Roberts students and the sixth-grade Laidlaw students improved significantly in the recognition of adverbs and adverbials.

TABLE 16-2

Means, Standard Deviations and t Ratios for 6th Grade Pre- and Post-Test Scores of Roberts and Laidlaw Students

	Roberts		Laidlaw	
	Pretest	Post-test	Pretest	Post-test
N	13	13	17	17
X	30.38	46.85	20.12	31.12
SD	2.82	2.51	5.56	9.53
t		3.86*		3.98*

*p<.01

TABLE 16-3

Analysis of Covariance for the Comparison of Growth Scores of Roberts and Laidlaw Students in 5th Grade

Source of Variance	df	Adjusted Sums of Squares	Mean Squares	F
Between Group	1	1421.25	1421.25	
Within Group	40	2421.25	60.528	
Total	41			23.48*

*p<.01

The data in Table 16-3 show that null hypothesis 5 was rejected at the .01 probability level. It therefore can be concluded that when individual scores were adjusted for I.Q., the fifth-grade Roberts pupils showed a more significant mean growth rate (F = 23.48, p <.01) in comparison with the fifth-grade Laidlaw pupils.

In Table 16-4, the failure to reject null hypothesis 6 (F = .79, p >.05), points out that the 13 sixth-grade Roberts pupils did not exhibit a more significant mean growth rate than the 17 Laidlaw pupils of the same grade when individual scores were adjusted for intelligence. It appears then that at the higher grade level both approaches are equally adequate, whereas at the fifth-grade level the Roberts' approach is more desirable, especially for children of above average intelligence. In considering such conclusions, however, one should keep in mind the study's limitations mentioned previously.

TABLE 16-4

Analysis of Covariance for the Comparison of Growth Scores of Roberts and Laidlaw Students in 6th Grade

Source of Variance	df	Adjusted Sums of Squares	Mean Squares	F
Between Group	1	18.99	18.99	
Within Group	27	647.49	23.98	
Total	28			.79**

**$p > .05$

CONCLUSIONS

This investigation arrived at the following conclusions.
1. Significant differences do exist between the pre- and post-test mean English unit scores of pupils exposed to fifth and sixth-grade Roberts instruction.
2. Significant differences also exist between the pre- and post-test mean English unit scores of fifth and sixth-grade pupils exposed to the Laidlaw program.
3. Fifth-grade pupils using Roberts materials exhibit a significantly greater mean growth rate than fifth-grade pupils exposed to the Laidlaw program when the effects due to intelligence are partialed out.
4. No significant difference exists between the mean English unit growth rate of sixth-grade pupils exposed to the Roberts' approach and the mean English unit growth rate of sixth-grade pupils exposed to the Laidlaw approach when the effects due to intelligence were partialed out.

As a result of the above, the researchers suggest that the Roberts Linguistics program appears to be the stronger of the two programs, independent of the intelligence classification of the student to whom it is presented. The investigators further point out that the data presented in this study suggest that the Roberts Linguistics program can be placed into any intermediate grade without prior exposure and without loss in academic growth. It must be remembered, however, that these suggestions are based solely on isolated units of the Roberts and Laidlaw programs using a relatively small and purposive sample of pupils. Thus the investigators suggest that suitable replications of this study be conducted on larger samples of intermediate grade students and on a variety of English units in order to determine if such findings can be more generalized. It is further suggested that such future research spend more time on the construction and empirical validation of testing instruments in order to avoid inadequate test ceilings apparent in this research.

Questions for Brownell-McMath article:
1. The authors state that "special care was taken to assure that the two tests were comparable in terms of average item difficulty." Does this mean that statistical comparisons are now legitimate between the two tests? If not, what else should have been done?
2. Why did the authors change their statistical model from the t test to analysis of covariance for the testing of null hypotheses 5 and 6?
3. The authors have suggested that, on the basis of their research, the Roberts Linguistics program appears to be the stronger of the two programs. Is such a conclusion justifiable? Clarify.
4. The authors claim that one of the limitations of the study was that item difficulties were not determined empirically. Why were they interested in determining item difficulties? How could they have determined them empirically?
5. Design a study which would allow one to determine with more confidence than did the Brownell-McMath study, which of the two approaches to Linguistics works better for grades 5 and 6 students in a particular school.

SECTION IV

ATTITUDES, VALUES AND INTEREST STUDIES

17

THE USE OF THE VIDEORECORDER FOR CHANGING THE SELF CONCEPTS OF TEACHERS

GARY G. BAKER
Hamilton-Wenham Public Schools
Hamilton, Massachusetts

INTRODUCTION

The hypothesis of this research was that teachers could and would change their concepts of themselves as teachers if given the opportunity to view their own teaching on television.

There is some evidence that teachers do improve if they are asked to observe their teaching on television with a supervisor who points out flaws and raises questions. It is also probably true that in such situations many teachers are apprehensive and feel threatened. The result in many schools has been that the video-recorder has become an ogreish machine to be avoided rather than used. Regardless of the justification, teachers feel that the videorecorder is being used by the administration more for evaluation and judgment than analysis and professional improvement. However, if a teacher could have a class taped and then observe the tape on her own, without anyone else involved except the technician, there would be little reason for feeling threatened; an exception to this would be if the teacher felt threatened by her own image. In cases where she would like others to see it for analysis purposes, she could keep the tape until a convenient time was found in which she was able to view it with a peer or a superior.

PURPOSE

In this study, there was no attempt to have any teachers or supervisors sit in on either the actual class being taped or the showing of the taped class. In fact, there was a deliberate effort to avoid such action. The rationale behind the research was that, if the hypothesis were supported, it could be assumed that the videorecorder, without a supervisor's "assistance," could be a valuable aid to the teacher in helping her to improve classroom presentations.

If, however, the null hypothesis that self concepts would not be changed held true, it would seem to be worthless for the purpose of teacher improvement to have a teacher observe her own teaching on television. Therefore, the aim or purpose of this study was to gather evidence that would help in determining whether the videorecorder could be used profitably as a non-threatening tool for teacher self-analysis.

METHOD

Fifty positively worded items were devised by the researcher to measure the "self concept" construct. The thirty items comprising the final instrument were considered by the researcher and three consulting associates to be the most valid items for determining "self concept." Appendix A lists the thirty items of the questionnaire.

Ten female teachers in a primary school (grades 1-3) of the Hamilton-Wenham Public Schools agreed to participate in the experiment. Each teacher was assured that her results would be kept confidential and that not even the researcher would be able to match responses with names. Initially the participants were asked to react to each of the items on the self concept questionnaire. For each item (e.g. "I do no unnecessary talking in class.") they were asked to respond by marking "strongly agree," "agree," "don't know," "disagree," or "strongly disagree." Each response was given a weight from 4 to 0. A "Strongly agree" response would receive a weight of 4 and a "strongly disagree" response would receive a weight of 0.

After reacting to the questionnaire, each teacher then taught an abbreviated 15 to 20 minute lesson with 5 to 8 students, along the lines of the micro-teaching situations used by Professor Dwight Allen, the present Dean of the School of Education at the University of Massachusetts. The idea is that the shortened time and reduced number of students would reduce the variables for analysis and make the viewing time less burdensome. It certainly seemed that a highly structured, short lesson with a few students would be ideal for this study. It was felt that now the focus could be on the effectiveness of the lesson, and that variables inherent to over-sized classrooms and all day teaching would not effect unduly the conclusions drawn from teachers' reviews of the videorecordings. Thus, the question becomes: "Is the teacher effective in the best of circumstances?"

An obvious factor of which this researcher had little control was that only one of the 10 teachers previously had instructed in front of a videotape camera. Teachers and students are bound to be a little more self-consious when a class is videotaped but many admitted that once they started the lesson they forgot the camera was in the room. The technician, in fact, left the room in most cases, leaving the camera focused on the class, so that only the teacher and the students were in the class. Another uncontrollable fact was that the teachers probably were a bit more conscientious in planning the lessons that they were to give for this videotape experience.

After her lesson was videotaped each teacher made an appointment to view the instruction. All but one of the 10 teachers were able to view a replay of their classes. After each teacher privately viewed her class on television, she was asked to complete the same self-concept questionnaire. The researcher was able to match pre experimental questionnaires with post experimental questionnaires by matching code letters used by the teachers.

A two-tailed test of significance was utilized since there was no presumption that their self concepts would be negative or positive, only that they would see some things about themselves which previously they did not realize. A *t* ratio for the differences between paired observations as outlined by Mode (1961) was computed to test the null hypothesis of no significant difference between the teachers' self concepts as teachers before the television experience and their self concepts after viewing a videotape of their teaching.

RESULTS

The *t* ratio of 3.61 reported in Table 17-1 enabled the researcher to reject the null hypothesis of no significant difference between pre and post experimental self concepts at the .01 probability level. This means that the average differences of 2.0 between the results of the pre and post self concept measures could occur by chance less than one time in a hundred. The negative value of the "d" column in Table 17-1 further indicated that the teachers, in general, improved their self concepts after viewing their own instruction.

It is interesting to note, that in 23 of the 30 statements, (77%), teachers tended to improve their self images. The most marked change was that teachers were more certain than ever that they did "no unnecessary talking in class" (Item 2). There was also a decided increase in self concepts in the areas of : showing "to be really listening to the children" (Item 1b); proceeding with "appropriate deliberation from point to point" (Item 18); receiving "feedback" (Item 20); and achieving "lesson objective without wasting time" (Item 26).

There were only four statements to which the response was more negative after the tape had been viewed. These statements were: "I try to answer the children's questions" (Item 5); "I encourage and stimulate discussion between students as well as between the students and teacher" (Item 21); "I show pleasure with students' expressed insights, even though they are not what I myself had planned to be discovered"

TABLE 17-1

t Ratio of Difference between Paired Observations

Pair	Pretest x	Post-test y	Difference (d = x−y)	d²	t = 3.61*
1	29	30	−1	1	
2	18	28	−10	100	
3	29	32	−3	9	
4	28	32	−4	16	
5	34	32	+2	4	
6	20	22	−2	4	
7	25	26	−1	1	
8	22	23	−1	1	
9	32	35	−3	9	
10	30	31	−1	1	
11	31	33	−2	4	
12	30	30	0	0	
13	27	28	−1	1	
14	25	27	−2	4	
15	31	33	−2	4	
16	30	35	−5	25	
17	27	31	−4	16	
18	26	31	−5	25	
19	31	32	−1	1	
20	28	33	−5	25	
21	27	25	+2	4	
22	33	30	+3	9	
23	32	31	+1	1	
24	26	26	0	0	
25	32	32	0	0	
26	24	29	−5	25	
27	25	29	−4	16	
28	28	29	−1	1	
29	31	35	−4	16	
30	27	29	−2	4	
Sum	838	899	−61	327	

*p<.01

(Item 22), and "I am flexible but don't allow tangents to predominate in a lesson" (Item 23).

All this appears to mean that the use of the videotape in the manner described does make a significant difference in the teachers' self concept, but that this difference tends to reinforce their behavior as teachers rather than to bring any aspect of their behavior into any serious question. Thus, although the hypothesis of change is reinforced it would appear that the change is in the direction of building confidence in their concepts of themselves as teachers. It would appear that if this were an important purpose the videorecorder could help teachers build confidence in themselves.

SPECULATIONS

In certain respects the results appear to be misleading. The tendency to concentrate on the good and overlook the weak points would seem to be a natural human tendency when a person faces up to herself as a teacher; indeed as a human being. Unless a person is forced to consider flaws in herself as a teacher and as a human being, and to have these flaws pointed out or at least questioned, the natural tendency is to ignore them for the sake of the ego.

Very few teachers are objective, critical analysts of themselves as teachers, just as very few are capable of an objective, perceptive psychological self-analysis. It might be that teachers do not see on television what and who they really are. Instead, they see the self-image they have built up over the years. Thus, they tend to focus on and appreciate those characteristics that reinforce their preconceived notions of themselves as teachers. The features that are not in accordance with the self-image are not recognized, do not seem important, or, are too frightening to admit. In short, my hypothesis is that McCluhan (1967) is so right is saying that "the medium is the message." The teachers who told me "I was great" and "I really liked what I saw" might have thought they were being facetious, but they weren't. Most of them do have a high regard for themselves as teachers and what they saw (as opposed to what others might have perceived) reinforced their self concept. My conclusion, therefore, is that if you want to use the television to help teachers gain confidence, let them look at themselves by themselves; but if you want them to recognize deficiencies in teaching behavior someone must be there, threat or not, to help them identify their "real selves." It is generally too much to expect individuals to comtemplate themselves as fallible people with identifiable faults as teachers. Genuine critiques have to be made by people without an ego on the line. Class analyses and critiques can be as frightening as any soul searching a person can do, but perhaps they are still necessary; for a person must achieve an objective evaluation before she can be expected to become more effective.

A question for further research might ask if television can be useful in helping teachers to improve if the viewing of the class and the following analysis are done with another person, such as a grade leader or principal.

Reference

McCluhan, M., & Fiore, Q. *The Medium is the Message.* New York: Random House, 1967.

Mode, E. *Elements of Statistics.* Englewood Cliffs, New Jersey: Prentice-Hall, Inc., 1961.

APPENDIX

Items Comprising Teacher Profile Questionnaire

1. I ask clear questions and give clear instructions.
2. I do no unnecessary talking in class.
3. I am patient with irrelevant questions from the children.
4. I am able to maintain a focus for discussion which is clearly related to my lesson objectives.
5. I try to answer the children's questions.
6. My voice is pleasing to others.
7. My manner and attitude in class are pleasing to others.
8. I have no habits or mannerisms which might be irritating to students.
9. I am firm in maintaining discipline but not unnecessarily stern.
10. The children appear to like me as a person.
11. I appear to like children.
12. I put the blackboard and/or audio-visual aids to good use in getting the children to focus on key ideas in the lessons.
13. I tolerate comments by students which are personal but not useful to the lesson.
14. I correct grammatical or pronunciation errors that students make immediately but tactfully.
15. I try to show the relevance of the lesson to the class.
16. I appear to be really listening to the children.
17. The children really appear to be listening to me when I talk.
18. I do not proceed from point to point too rapidly for the children or before I am sure they understand each stage in the lesson.
19. I summarize or have students summarize the major points of the lesson at logical points, including the end.
20. I receive enough feedback to know whether the children have learned what I hoped they would.
21. I encourage and stimulate discussion among students as well as between the students and teacher.
22. I show pleasure with students' expressed insights, even though they are not what I myself had planned to be discovered.
23. I am flexible but don't allow tangents to predominate in a lesson.
24. I seem to have a sense of humor.

25. I seem to appreciate the children's humor.
26. I seem to be able to achieve my lesson objectives without wasting time.
27. The children seem to understand the purpose of the lesson from the beginning.
28. I am sensitive to intellectual and emotional subtleties which students hint at and I help them to develop their perceptions more fully in oral terms.
29. I give all of the students the opportunity to participate in the lesson.
30. I have all the technical tools and proper attitude which make a good teacher.

Questions on the Baker study.
1. In what ways does this study lack internal validity?
2. In what ways does this study lack external validity?
3. Why did the author choose a two tailed test of significance? How does this differ from a one tailed test?
4. The author chose to test his null hypothesis by computing a t ratio for the differences between paired observations. What is unusual about the author's choice of "pairs" in contrast to what such a significance test would normally assume for "pairs?"
5. Has this study proven that videotapes can help teachers critically analyze their teaching? If not, what has it proven?
6. Could you suggest a better way in which the author could have tested his null hypothesis?

18

HIGH SCHOOL ENGLISH AND SOCIAL SCIENCE CURRICULA OF ONE SEMESTER ELECTIVE COURSES: DO STUDENTS AND TEACHERS THINK THEY ARE BETTER THAN THE TRADITIONAL CURRICULA OF FULL YEAR NON-ELECTIVE COURSES?

JOHN C. HAVICE
North Reading High School
North Reading, Massachusetts

In order to serve better the needs and interests of the students at North Reading High School, the English and Social Sciences Departments revised their program of studies from the traditional full year courses, that were primarily non-elective, to one semester all-elective courses. The new curricula have been in operation in the English and Social Sciences Departments for two years and one year respectively. Comments by administrators, teachers, and students seemed to indicate that the new program, with few exceptions, has been a success. Until this time no actual research study had been attempted to determine the extent of favorable acceptance or effectiveness of the new curricula at North Reading High School. Because of the impossibility, at the time this study was conducted, of establishing control and experimental groups to measure achievement, only research measuring attitudes toward the program was feasible this year. Consequently, we attempted to learn if the attitudes toward the present curricula were more favorable than toward the former curricula.

PURPOSE

The purpose of this investigation was to determine whether the attitudes of students and teachers are significantly more favorable toward the present curricula than toward the former curricula. If the attitudes are significantly more favorable, the value of the program will have been proven, in part, by the degree of its acceptance.

The degree of acceptance is indicated by the level at which the null hypothesis can be rejected. The null hypothesis tested was: Attitudes of students and teachers toward the program of one semester elective courses in the English and Social Sciences Departments are not significantly more favorable than toward the traditional program of full year non-elective courses.

SAMPLE AND INSTRUMENT

This study used for its testing sample 90 out of a total of 608 upper class students. Each teacher in both departments selected at random from each of the upper grades 5 students he currently had in his own classes. From the lists of these students, 30 students from each of the three upper classes were selected at random. These 90 students appeared to represent a good cross-section of academic and non-academic abilities and interests. Each teacher in both departments was asked to submit 10 statements that he thought were most relevant to the program. From these statements, the 25 most pertinent ones were chosen for the questionnaire by a panel of judges. The students were asked to indicate the degree to which they agreed with the statements by placing a check mark in boxes labeled "strongly agree," "agree," "disagree" and "strongly disagree." All statements were worded as positive statements since it was felt that some students might be confused if positive and negative statements were used. However, students were warned in the directions, both orally and written, that all statements were worded as positive statements, but, that they should read each statement carefully before deciding upon an agree or disagree response. Hopefully such directions guarded against the students falling into a positive response set.

Because positive or negative trends for each statement and for the questionnaire in general were desired, no neutral response, such as "undecided" or "sometimes agree and sometimes disagree," was allowed.

The faculty members of both departments were given a similar questionnaire. While some wording of statements was necessarily changed, the intent of the statements was not changed. (Appendicies A and B contain the questions of both instruments.)

DESIGN

The chi square test was used in testing the null hypothesis that attitudes toward the present curricula are not significantly more favorable than toward the former curricula. This null hypothesis was first tested on the basis of the student attitudes and secondly on the basis of the teacher attitudes. To determine the degree of significance, the level at which the null hypothesis can be rejected must be known. The lower the percentage level at which the null hypothesis can be rejected, the

142 | ATTITUDES, VALUES AND INTEREST STUDIES

greater will be the degree of favorable significance, and the less possibility that the results occurred by chance alone.

Point values of 3, 2, 1, and 0 were assigned to the responses "strongly agree," "agree," "disagree," and "strongly disagree," respectively. The number of points for each questionnaire were totaled. The total number of points for each questionnaire could range from 75 (3 points per "strongly agree" response for each 25 statements) down to 0 (0 points per "strongly disagree" response for each of the 25 statements). By chance alone, it would be expected that each questionnaire would have a total of 37.5 points (one half of the responses answered favorably and the other half of the responses answered negatively), if there were no difference in attitudes, either favorably or negatively, toward the present curricula.

RESULTS

Point values were assigned for each response and totaled for each questionnaire. The breakdown by class for students whose total points were either above or below 37.5 is shown in Table 18-1.

TABLE 18-1

Number of Students in Each Class with Point Totals Above and Below 37.5

	Above 37.5	Below 37.5
Seniors	30	0
Juniors	26	4
Sophomores	29	1
Totals	85	5

It would be expected by chance alone that 45 of the students would have a total number of points above 37.5 and that 45 students would have a total number of points below 37.5. That is, by chance alone, half of the students would like the present program better and the other half of the students would not like the present curricula better than the former one.

The results reported in Table 18-2 show that 85 students had a total number of points above 37.5, whereas 45 were expected to by chance. Also, five students had a total number of points below 37.5, whereas 45 were expected to by chance.

TABLE 18-2

Observed and Expected Frequencies of Student Totals Above and Below 37.5

Groups	Observed Frequency	Expected Frequency	chi square
Above 37.5 (positive attitude)	85	45	54.44*
Below 37.5 (negative attitude)	5	45	

*$p < .001$

Since the computed chi square of 54.44 was far beyond the value of 10.827 necessary to reach significance at the 0.1% level, the null hypothesis of no significant difference between observed and expected frequency of the positive and negative student groups, was rejected at the 0.1% level. Thus Table 18-2 indicates that the attitudes of students are significantly more favorable toward the present curricula than the former one. Put another way, less than one time in 1000 these attitudinal responses to the questionnaire could occur by chance alone.

The results of questionnaires completed by teachers showed that 12 teachers had a total number of points above 37.5 while three teachers had point totals below 37.5. Also, 12 teachers had a total number of points above 37.5, whereas 7.5 were expected to by chance. Three teachers had point totals below 37.5 whereas 7.5 were expected to by chance.

As the value necessary for significance at the 5% level is 3.841 and the computed chi square value was 5.400, Table 18-4, therefore, indi-

TABLE 18-3

Number of Teachers in Each Department with Point Totals Above and Below 37.5

	Above 37.5	Below 37.5
English	7	1
Social Sciences	5	2
Totals	12	3

TABLE 18.4

Observed and Expected Frequencies of Teacher Totals Above and Below 37.5

Groups	Observed Frequency	Expected Frequency	chi square
Above 37.5	12	7.5	5.40*
Below 37.5	3	7.5	

*$p<.05$

cates that the null hypothesis can be rejected at the 5% level. Such a conclusion was not altered when the computed chi square was corrected for continuity. Therefore, the attitudes of teachers are significantly more favorable toward the present curricula than toward the former curricula. Put another way, such significant positive attitudes of the teachers toward the new curricula could occur by chance only, five times in 100.

The chi square results have shown that the attitudes of upper class students and teachers in the English and Social Sciences Departments are significantly more favorable toward the curricula of one semester elective courses in both departments than toward the former full year non-elective curricula.

At this point the researcher attempted to determine the major reasons for such positive student and teacher attitudes toward the new curricula by considering those items in the questionnaire in which specific positive attitudes were most apparent. Tables 18-5 and 18-6 indicate the student and teacher responses to the 25 items.

The reasons indicated most frequently why students preferred the present curricula were: (1) the courses are more interesting; (2) students have more of a say in the course they can take; (3) there is more student discussion and less lecturing by the teacher; (4) the courses provide a greater awareness and understanding of international, national, state, and local problems; (5) students can study specific topic courses rather than general survey courses; and (6) high school is a more worthwhile experience as a result of the present curricula. Table 18-5 summarizes the student responses to each statement.

The reasons indicated most frequently why the faculty members in both departments preferred the present curricula were: (1) the courses are more interesting; (2) teachers feel that students have more of a say

TABLE 18-5
Frequency Distribution for Student Questionnaire

Item No.	Strongly Agree	Agree	Disagree	Strongly Disagree
1.	43	44	3	0
2.	18	54	14	4
3.	19	37	23	11
4.	13	53	20	4
5.	7	36	41	6
6.	23	49	16	2
7.	29	47	12	2
8.	23	49	14	4
9.	26	47	15	2
10.	16	37	34	3
11.	29	38	17	6
12.	14	36	35	5
13.	26	47	15	2
14.	4	35	46	5
15.	12	47	24	7
16.	26	40	21	3
17.	34	42	11	3
18.	35	40	11	4
19.	49	37	2	2
20.	29	48	12	1
21.	19	39	21	11
22.	15	30	33	12
23.	24	47	18	1
24.	13	46	26	5
25.	47	35	4	4

in what courses they can take; (3) the courses provide a greater awareness and understanding of international, national, state, and local problems; (4) the courses are generally more related to current times; and (5) paperback books are used more often than traditional textbooks. Table 18-6 summarizes the faculty responses to each statement.

IMPLICATIONS

It should be restated that this study reflects only attitudes and does not measure achievement resulting from both curricula. One might assume, however, that achievement is likely to be greater when attitudes are favorable. What this study has shown is that upper class students and teachers in both departments feel that the present program in those departments are more worthwhile than the traditional program of full year non-elective courses. It appears then, that the results

ATTITUDES, VALUES AND INTEREST STUDIES

TABLE 18-6
Frequency Distribution for Faculty Questionnaire

Item No.	Strongly Agree	Agree	Disagree	Strongly Disagree
1.	10	5	0	0
2.	6	9	0	0
3.	4	3	7	1
4.	3	11	1	0
5.	2	4	7	2
5.	2	4	7	2
7.	6	6	3	0
8.	2	10	3	0
9.	2	6	5	2
10.	3	8	4	0
11.	0	6	8	1
12.	5	8	2	0
13.	5	7	3	0
14.	2	7	4	2
15.	2	9	4	0
16.	4	11	0	0
17.	6	9	0	0
18.	6	8	1	0
19.	6	9	0	0
20.	3	9	3	0
21.	0	3	8	4
22.	1	3	7	4
23.	4	8	3	0
24.	2	8	4	1
25.	7	7	1	0

of this study suggest that the present program is better able to meet the needs and interests of the students.

One reason why the significance level was not as high for the teachers group might be that the teachers felt that some of the college bound students were electing "easier" courses, ones that require less effort by the student or were less challenging intellectually.

The study indicates that while students and teachers liked elective courses, both students and teachers were in strong agreement that some of the non-elective courses in the former curricula should be required for all students in a particular grade or program of study. Further research would be helpful here.

A further implication of the study is that curricula containing some one semester elective courses may be desirable for other subject areas as well as for English and Social Sciences. For example, the Science

Department at North Reading High School is considering implementing some one semester elective courses.

Reference

Siegel, S., *Nonparametric statistics for the behavioral sciences.* New York: McGraw-Hill, 1956.

APPENDIX A

Questions Contained in North Reading Research Study Student Questionnaire

1. Courses in the present curricula are generally more interesting.
2. The present curricula are better because I can change courses more frequently.
3. Being grouped with students of varying abilities is better than being grouped with students of the same ability.
4. The present curricula are better because I can change teachers more frequently.
5. More reading and studying are required of me than in the former curricula.
6. Courses in the present curricula are generally more related to current times.
7. In English and Social Science it is better to study specific topic courses, such as those in the present curricula, rather than general survey courses, such as those in the traditional curricula.
8. The present curricula prepare the student for schooling or work after high school better than the former non-elective curricula.
9. I choose the courses that I do more because of a sincere interest in those courses than because they are easier or just fun.
10. The present curricula are better because I can choose my teachers.
11. I choose the courses that I do more because of a sincere interest in those courses than because I can be with my friends.
12. Teachers of the present curricula have become better teachers because of the new curricula.
13. I have become more curious intellectually with the present curricula than with the former curricula.
14. I have developed better study habits with the present curricula than with the former curricula.
15. The courses in the present curricula are adequately covered in one semester.
16. The present curricula are better because paperback books are used more often than traditional textbooks.
17. The present curricula provide a greater awareness and understanding of international, national, state, and local problems.

148 | ATTITUDES, VALUES AND INTEREST STUDIES

18. I become more involved in my classes in the present curricula than I did in the traditional courses.
19. The present curricula are better because I have more of a say in what courses I can take.
20. In class there is generally more student discussion and less lecturing by the teacher in the present curricula.
21. None of the elective courses in the present curricula should be required courses that all students in a particular grade or program of study should have to take.
22. None of the non-elective courses in the former curricula should be required courses that all students in a particular grade or program of study should have to take.
23. I feel that my ability to communicate with others, talking, and in writing, has improved more with the present curricula.
24. I feel that my reading speed and understanding of what I read have improved more with the present curricula.
25. I feel that, in general, high school is a more worthwhile experience as a result of the present curricula.

APPENDIX B

Questions Contained in North Reading Research Study Teacher Questionnaire

1. Courses in the present curricula are generally more interesting.
2. The present curricula are better because students can change courses more frequently.
3. Grouping of students of varying abilities is better than grouping of students of the same ability.
4. The present curricula are better because students can change teachers more frequently.
5. More reading and studying are required of students than in the former curricula.
6. Courses in the present curricula are generally more related to current times.
7. In English and Social Science it is better to study specific topic courses, such as those in the present curricula, rather than general survey courses, such as those in the traditional curricula.
8. The present curricula prepare the student for schooling or work after high school better than the former non-elective curricula.
9. Students choose the courses that they do more because of a sincere interest in those courses than because they are easier or just fun.

10. The present curricula are better because students can choose their teachers.
11. Students choose the courses that they do more because of a sincere interest in those courses than because students can' be with their friends.
12. Teachers of the present curricula have become better teachers because of the new curricula.
13. Students have become more curious intellectually with the present curricula than with the former curricula.
14. Students have developed better study habits with the present curricula than with the former curricula.
15. The courses in the present curricula are adequately covered in one semester.
16. The present curricula are better because paperback books are used more often than traditional textbooks.
17. The present curricula provide a greater awareness and understanding of international, national, state, and local problems.
18. Students have become more involved in their classes in the present curricula than they did in the traditional courses.
19. The present curricula are better because students have more of a say in what courses they can take.
20. In class there is generally more student discussion and less lecturing by the teacher in the present curricula.
21. None of the elective courses in the present curricula should be required courses that all students in a particular grade or program of study should have to take.
22. None of the non-elective courses in the former curricula should be required courses that all students in a particular grade or program of study should have to take.
23. The ability of students to communicate with others, talking and in writing, has improved more with the present curricula.
24. The reading speed of students and understanding of what they read have improved more with the present curricula.
25. I feel that, in general, high school is a more worthwhile experience for students as a result of the present curricula.

Questions on the Havice article.
1. What is meant by the following statement made by the author in the third paragraph of the study: "The degree of acceptance is indicated by the level at which the null hypothesis can be rejected."?
2. How did the author attempt to assure that his attitude instrument had content validity? Suggest another method he could have used.

3. Exactly what does the author mean by a positive response set?
4. The author reported a chi square value of 54.44 significant at the 0.1% level. What is a more traditional way of reporting this same result?
5. What is meant by the statement "... chi square was corrected for continuity."?
6. In what ways do the faculty and students agree that the new curricula are better?
7. Do you feel that the author has done a service for his school? Justify your answer.

19

A COMPARISON OF READING PREFERENCE OF SECOND GRADE STUDENTS AND PARENT'S SELECTION OF CHILDREN'S LITERATURE

David W. Hilton
Worcester State College
Worcester, Massachusetts

and

Judith A. Shepard
Mary D. Stone Elementary School
Auburn, Massachusetts

INTRODUCTION

The purpose of this research was to determine to what extent choices of reading matter selected by children would correspond to selections of reading matter chosen for children by their parents. A substantial amount of research has been conducted which shows that children of each sex have substantially different interests in reading dependent on the subject matter to be read.

In a study similar to this done at the intermediate elementary level, Jefferson (1958) found that parents appreciated the importance of animals, children, and magic in stories for girls, and the appeal of real animals and adventure in boys' stories. Harris (1955) conducted a study of 248 first grade children and concluded that girls were most interested in stories involving children, romance, and marriage, while boys chose stories about adult adventure and exciting events. A study of 275 first graders (Rogers and Robinson, 1962) resulted with girls choosing areas of interest concerned with fantasy, home life, and romance, while boys selected stories with adventurous and historical themes.

Since sex differences in reading interest apparently exist as early as the first grade, and probably before, it should be of interest to discover whether parents are realistic in their choices of literature for their children, since parents select almost all of their reading material before school age and a substantial amount in the early elementary grades. The following null hypotheses were specifically tested:

$1H_o$ —There is no significant correlation of the selections of reading matter made by male, second grade students and those made by their parents for them.

$2H_o$ —There is no significant correlation of the selections of reading matter made by female, second grade students and those made by their parents for them.

$3H_o$ —There is no significant difference in the correlations of choice of reading matter in relation to the sex of the child for which the reading matter is chosen.

PROCEDURE

For this study, a questionnaire was devised consisting of thirty fictitious titles and annotations. Fictitious titles were used to preclude selections based on stories students had actually read and on which they had formed judgements. Examples of the annotated story titles are:

Mystery in the Dark Woods: Mrs. Rabbit disappeared without clue. The animals play detective to find her.
Shipwrecked on the Moon: The tale of the crew of the *Star 3* and their adventure on the moon.

An effort was made to include a wide variety of reading interest areas: fantasy, romance, children, animals, historical themes, etc. As each story title and annotation was read, the students were asked to circle *no,* if he did not want to read the book, *?* if he was uncertain whether he would like to read the book, or *yes* if he felt that he would like to read the book. Each child brought the questionnaire home with instructions to parents which stated that they should respond to the questionnaire with regard to what they felt their son or daughter would like to read. They were to respond without asking their children for their preferences.

Thirty-one children were given the questionnaire, 14 girls and 17 boys. Of the 14 girls, one was discarded because she circled *yes* to every story title, and of the 17 boys, one was discarded because he circled two choices for every title. Of the 31 questionnaires sent home, one was returned without designating whether the student for which the choices were made was male or female.

The story titles were ranked separately for each of the four groups: male students, female students, parents of male students, and parents of female students. Each *yes* was given a weight of 3 points, a *?* response weighted 2 points and a *no* weighted 1 point. The story title with the greatest point value for each group was ranked 1, the second greatest point value was ranked 2, and so forth. In the case of ties, the usual system of averaging the ranks was used. A Spearman Rank-Order correlation was then computed between rankings of female students and their parents, and similarly for male students rankings and their parents.

RESULTS

Table 19-1 shows the rankings of the thirty fictitious story titles for each of the four groups described. The correlation, rho, between female students' preferences and those of their parents was computed to be

TABLE 19-1

Rankings of Thirty Fictitious Story Titles by Second Students and their Parents

Story Titles	Female Students	Parents of Females	Male Students	Parents of Males
The Magic Pebbles	1	7	23	11
Making a Birthday Cake	3	7	29.5	29.5
Easy Arithmetic	3	13	2	21
Anette	3	3	20.5	25
The Cow who Took a Walk	6	3	2	14
Rosa, the Mexican Girl	6	3	29.5	28
Mystery in the Dark Woods	6	15	23	16.5
Mary the Nurse	8.5	7	26.5	26.5
The Magic Loafers	8.5	3	28	29.5
Pick a Joke	11.5	11	7.5	29.5
Happy Leonard	11.5	3	10	2
Red Fox and his Boat	11.5	17	16.5	11
Larger Giant	11.5	18.5	12.5	6.5
Harvey the Tiger	14.5	15	12.5	1
The Magic Violin	14.5	11	26.5	24
Harry the Fireman	16	11	16.5	3
Alice and the Elephant	17	9	20.5	26.5
A Tale of Bob Cat	18.5	15	7.5	19
Noodlehead	18.5	21.5	25	22
What Do Animals Do?	20	18.5	16.5	4
Shipwrecked on the Moon	21	23	5.5	6.5
Kites	22	25	16.5	16.5
Airplanes	23	27	4	11
Famous U. S. Naval Battles	25	28	10	23
Beetles, Bugs, and Bees	25	24	10	11
Three Boys and a Helicopter	25	26	5.5	6.5
A Boat for Peppet	27	20	16.5	16.5
Clem	28	21.5	23	11
A Story of Weapons	29	30	16.5	20
Motors That You Can Make	30	29	2	6.5

+ 0.85; the correlation between male students' preferences and parents of these students was + 0.56. Both of these correlations are significantly different from 0.0 at the .01 level.

The difference between these two correlations was significant at the .01 level also. All three of the null hypotheses, then, were rejected.

DISCUSSION

It seems apparent that, while parents of both male and female second grade students are knowledgeable of reading interests of their children, parents have a better idea of the preferences of their daughters than of their sons. The authors find no obvious reason why this should be so. It may be, however, that the questionnaires were filled out predominantly by the students' mothers, rather than their fathers (no directions on the questionnaire specified which parent was to respond). A quick glance at the rankings of story titles made by female students versus male students corroborates evidence cited earlier in this paper that reading interests have become substantially differentiated according to sex in the early elementary grades. A repetition of this study is presently underway at the pre-school level which will attempt to discover at what age this differentiation becomes noticeable.

References

DeBoer, John J., and Martha Dallmann. *The Teaching of Reading.* New York: Holt, Rinehart and Winston, 1965.

Huck, Charlotte S., and Doris A. Young. *Children's Literature in the Elementary School.* New York: Holt, Rinehart and Winston, 1966.

Jefferson, Benjamin F. "Some Relationships Between Parents and Children's Preference," *Elementary School Journal,* 58 (1958), 212-218.

Rogers, Helen, and H. Alan Robinson. "Reading Interests of First Graders," *Elementary English,* 40 (1963), 707-712.

Zimet, Sara F. "Children's Interest and Story Preferences: A Critical Review of the Literature," *Elementary School Journal,* 67 (1966), 122-130.

Questions on the Hilton and Shepard article.

1. Was the sample size in this study large enough to provide an adequate rating of the story titles?
2. Only one class of students was used. Is it possible that very different results would have been obtained had a different class been used?
3. Would it make a difference in terms of which parent did the rating of the story titles?
4. From Table 19-1, what is your prediction of the correlation between rankings of male and female second grade students?
5. In response to question 4, would such a correlation be helpful in interpreting the results of this study?

20

A STUDY OF TRADITIONAL AND EMERGENT VALUES OF EIGHTH GRADE STUDENTS IN THREE ACADEMIC GROUPS

DAVID H. QUIST and DAVID W. HILTON
Worcester State College
Worcester, Massachusetts

INTRODUCTION

Seldom in American history has the public been as concerned, as it is today, with student values. Many feel the traditional way of life is eroding as today's youth, in increasing numbers, question time honored moral and social value systems. Parents find that they are unable to communicate with their children; children are bewildered by the beliefs and actions of their parents who are "square" or "not with it." The value gap between teachers and students is also more noticeable now than at any time in the past. Students argue that the schools must change with the times while many teachers maintain that some traditional values are as important today as they were a hundred years ago.

Students are affected by values and value patterns in many ways, some more subtle than others. Rist (1970), in a recent article in the *Harvard Education Review,* found that kindergarten and first grade teachers made decisions about the success or failure of their students based upon the child's social class and value system. Once the initial classification is made, the self fulfilling prophecy begins to operate. The "fast" learner, the student who accepts the teacher's values, get more attention and help, while the "slow" learner is often neglected. Similar studies by Battle (1957), Prince (1957), and Thompson (1965, 1968) have resulted in the same basic conclusions.

This study was an attempt to discover whether the traditional values usually applauded by teachers, or the newer emergent values of the youth of this generation, are discernible in different degrees in relation to the ability group in which the student is placed.

PROCEDURE

An instrument designed to measure Traditional and Emergent values was constructed to measure the following dimensions:

Traditional Values

Puritan Morality: Respectability, thrift, self-denial, sexual constraint, respect for elders, feelings of guilt.

Work Success Ethic: Successful people work hard to become so. Anyone can get to the top if he tries hard enough. Success is a constant goal. There is no resting on past glories. People must work desperately and continuously to convince themselves of their worth.

Individualism: The individual is sacred and always more important than the group. In one extreme form, this value sanctions egocentricity, expediency, and disregard for other people's rights. In its healthier form, the value sanctions independence and originality.

Future Time Orientation: The future, not the past or even the present, is most important. Time is valuable and cannot be wasted. *Present needs* must be denied for satisfaction to be gained in the future.

Emergent Values

Sociability: One should like people and get along well with them. Solitary activities are looked upon with suspicion.

Relativistic Morality: Absolutes in right and wrong are questionable. Morality is what the group thinks is right or according to personal conscience.

Conformity: Everything is relative to the group. Group harmony is the ultimate goal. Everything one does should be done with regard for others and their feelings.

Present Time Orientation: No one can tell what the future will hold; therefore, one should enjoy the present, within the limits of what is prescribed for the well-rounded, balanced personality. The emphasis is on spending money and having fun.

The instrument described above was administered to 305 eighth grade students in a predominantly middle-class school. Of the total number, 130 students were in the highest or "honors" group, 136 were in the "college" group and 39 were in the "general," the lowest academic group. Each of the 8 value scales contained the same number of questions which were responded to on a four point, agree strongly-disagree strongly, scale. The responses were dichotomized for this study to provide a simple agree-disagree response scale. In all cases, an agree response was scored as an acceptance of the value described and given the greater weight. A total score for each of the major dimensions, Traditional and Emergent, was obtained by adding the four value scale scores defined under each dimension. A one way analysis of variance by academic group was computed for each of the eight value scales and the two total scale scores. A generalized ANOVA (ANalysis Of VAriance) computer program was used to account for the different n's in each academic group.

RESULTS

Table 20-1 shows the means and standard deviations of the eight value scale scores and the two total scale scores for each of the three academic groups.

TABLE 20-1

Means and Standard Deviations of Eighth Grade Students on Traditional and Emergent Value Scales Compared by Academic Group

Value Scale	Honors Mean	Honors S.D.	College Mean	College S.D.	General Mean	General S.D.
Traditional Values						
Puritan Morality	9.18	1.78	8.74	2.20	8.15	2.63
Work Success Ethic	9.41	2.07	9.43	2.01	8.97	2.46
Individualism	9.50	1.42	9.29	1.82	8.82	1.68
Future Time Orientation	10.48	1.55	9.84	1.95	9.20	2.42
Total Scale	38.56	4.74	37.30	5.38	35.15	7.40
Emergent Values						
Sociability	10.61	1.58	10.26	1.58	9.31	2.29
Relativistic Morality	4.76	2.37	5.21	2.50	4.44	2.07
Conformity	2.90	1.95	3.94	2.41	3.67	2.39
Present Time Orientation	7.55	1.56	7.49	1.89	7.38	2.28
Total Scale	25.82	4.57	26.90	5.73	24.80	6.16

Table 20-2 shows the results of the analysis of variance for each of the 10 measures. In conjunction with Table 20-1, these results indicate that values described under *Puritan Morality* and *Future Time Orientation* significantly increase from the lowest to the highest academic group. The total scale values for the *Traditional Values* dimension shows a similar correspondence and was significant at the .05 level. Values described under the *Individualism* scale show the same pattern of increase but the observed differences were not significant at the .05 level. *Work Success Ethic* values appear to be least important in characterizing the three groups.

On the *Emergent* dimension, *Sociability* shows the same increase from low to high academic group. Conformity, however, does not appear to be linearly related to the academic group; the highest average was obtained by the middle academic group. On the *Relativistic Morality* scale, the *Present Time Orientation* scale, and the total scale scores on this dimension, no significant differences were found.

TABLE 20-2

Analysis of Variance of Traditional and Emergent Value Scores of Eighth Grade Students in Three Academic Groups

Value Scale	Among Sum of Squares (df = 2)	Within Sum of Squares (df = 302)	Among Mean Square	Within Mean Square	F
Traditional					
Puritan Morality	34.58	1340.48	17.29	4.44	3.90*
Work Success Ethic	6.83	1343.77	3.42	4.45	0.77
Individualism	14.03	824.48	7.02	2.73	2.57
Future Time Orientation	57.50	1057.23	28.75	3.50	8.21**
Total Scale	365.28	8999.72	182.64	29.80	6.13*
Emergent					
Sociability	50.84	867.77	25.42	2.87	8.85**
Relativistic Morality	23.52	1747.43	11.76	5.79	2.03
Conformity	73.92	1509.90	36.96	5.00	7.39**
Present Time Orientation	0.90	1005.35	0.45	3.33	0.13
Total Scale	162.74	8669.05	81.37	28.70	2.83

*Significant at the .05 level of probability.
**Significant at the .01 level of probability.

DISCUSSION

Of the various findings, the least disputable would appear to be the significantly higher acceptance of traditional values by the higher academic groups. A question which still remains is whether the better students accept these values after embarking on their formal education or simply have such values as a result of parental training. In either case, the student who accepts traditional values of hard work and delayed gratification appears to have an edge on the student who fails to accept such values.

Some of the results might appear to be in contradiction to each other; while *Future Time Orientation* values were accepted in greater numbers by the higher academic groups, *Present Time Orientation* values show the pattern of increase. Since the items written for the two scales measure different ends of the continuum of time orientation, one might expect the opposite result. While it is possible that the questions used were not actually measuring this continuum, it is also possible that students are pulled in both directions at the same time; the student who wishes to achieve must accept traditional values in order to do so, but also desires to be part of the larger peer group that tends to accept the newer values.

The importance of students' values cannot be overstated. The schools of today face a difficult challenge: to reinforce the values which have traditionally been successful in developing achievement, or to radically change the school environment in order to make a place for students who accept different value systems. Since education as an institution has usually shown itself reluctant to make drastic changes, the future may show still greater disaffection of the students with the school. "Dropping out and turning on" may be the only alternative for tomorrow's youth.

References

Battle, H. "Relation between personal values and scholastic achievement," *Journal of Experimental Education,* 1957, 26, 27-41.

Prince, Richard. *A Study of the Relationship between individual values and administrative effectiveness in the school situation.* Unpublished Ph.D. dissertation, University of Chicago, 1957.

Rist, Ray. "Student social class and teacher expectations: the self-fulfilling prophecy in ghetto education," *Harvard Educational Review,* 1970. 40, 411-451.

Thompson, O. E. "High school students and their values," *California Journal of Educational Research,* 1965, 16, 216-227.

Thompson, O. E. "Student values in transition," *California Journal of Educational Research,* 1968, 19, 77-86.

Questions on the Quist and Hilton article.

1. While teachers were not the focus of this study, with which of the two value dimensions do you suppose they would be most in agreement?
2. Which of the traditional values was most significant in discriminating the three academic groups? Can you justify your answer from the data presented in this study?
3. What inferences can be made from this middle class population to other non-middle class groups?
4. What other scales might have been included in either of the two major dimensions?
5. How might one account for the apparent nonlinear relationship of conformity by academic group?

21

THE VALUE OF KUDER INTEREST PROFILES OF TRADE SCHOOL BOYS FOR COUNSELING

MARY H. SHANN
Boston University
Boston, Massachasetts

Inventoried measures of interests have been used to a considerable extent by high school guidance counselors as a major source of information about motivational aspects of academic and vocational behavior. A substantial body of research validates this application of interest scores as a means of offering students direction in selecting and preparing for careers.

A comprehensive, longitudinal study of the relationship between *Kuder Preference Record—Vocational,* Form C (1959) profiles obtained in high school and subsequent job satisfaction responses seven to 10 years later, was undertaken by McRae (1959). McRae's study indicated that individuals who enter occupations consistent with their interests as measured when they were in high school were more likely to be satisfied with their work. Earlier cross-sectional studies of specific homogeneous occupational groups also revealed definite positive correlations between Kuder interest profiles and job satisfaction (Brayfield, 1946; DiMichael and Dabelstein, 1947; Hahn and Williams, 1945; Jacobs and Traxler, 1954; and North, 1958).

Mierzwa (1961) conducted research on the value of aptitude, achievement, social status, temperament, and interest measures for distinguishing between male students who had selected science versus non-science careers. He found that the interest dimension as measured by the Kuder was most capable of discriminating between the two groups.

In a study of male college preparatory students, Madaus and O'Hara (1967) demonstrated that vocational choice crystallized during the high school years and that this crystallization of vocational preference was more specific than the science-nonscience dichotomy found by Mierzwa. Using Kuder profiles to classify students according to their vocational choice, Madaus and O'Hara found that they were able to make correct classifications at rates well above those expected by chance.

Extending this promising vein of research, Mooney (1969) demonstrated that occupational group separations more specific than science-nonscience were also possible for college preparatory high school girls. On the basis of *Kuder E General Interest Survey* (1964) profiles, Mooney was able to classify subjects into eight broad vocational preference groups at almost five times the rate expected by chance. Furthermore, he crossvalidated this result on a similar sample.

The extensive body of research on the relationship between Kuder interest patterns and job satisfaction is, nevertheless, somewhat limited in that it deals almost exclusively with professional and semiprofessional groups who seem to be most satisfied with their work (Kuder, 1964, p. 39). Similarly, studies of the value of Kuder scores for predicting vocational preference are based on college preparatory subjects, most of whom will enter professional and other higher level business positions.

PURPOSE

This study attempted to extend the work of previous investigators by focusing on the value of Kuder interests as a means of counseling trade school boys, the potential skilled workers. The researcher attempted to answer the following questions: first, do the Kuder profiles of trade school students reveal characteristic likes and dislikes in ten broad interest areas measured by the Kuder instrument? Second, can differences in Kuder profiles be found among these subjects classified into seven groups according to the trade for which they had elected to train in school?

SAMPLE

Subjects of this study were 722 ninth- through twelfth-grade boys enrolled at two vocational high schools in New England. Each boy was classified according to his choice of trade into one of the following seven groups: auto mechanic, carpentry, electrical, machine, metal fabrication, plumbing, printing. The mean scores for these students on the *Otis-Lennon Mental Ability Test* (1967) was 101.8, while the standard deviation was 9.0. The vast majority of these boys emanated from blue-collar socioeconomic backgrounds.

INSTRUMENT

The *Kuder E General Interest Survey* (1964) was administered to subjects in small group sessions. This instrument provided inventoried measures of each subjects' interests in the following 10 broad interest areas: outdoor, mechanical, computational, scientific, persuasive, artistic, literary, musical, social service and clerical. The Kuder E Profile Leaflet (1963) suggested that interest scores falling at or beyond the highest and lowest quartiles, determined on the basis of appropriate norms, denote likes and dislikes that differentiate an individual's particular interests from those of most people of his grade level and sex across the nation. Scores falling between the 25th and 75th percentiles indicate interests which are about average compared to the norm group.

RESULTS

Distribution of Profile Scores

Studies by Samuelson (1958) on a sample of 58 vocational high school students and by Motto (1959) on a sample of 80 veterans enrolled in vocational training courses both reported "flat" Kuder profiles, characterized by an absence of scores falling at or beyond the first and third quartiles, for their subjects. Both researchers concluded that the Kuder instrument did not reveal patterns of each subject's particular likes and dislikes. However, this conclusion drawn in both independent investigations was unwarranted because it was based on inappropriate statistical techniques. Samuelson computed the mean of his entire sample for each Kuder scale and subsequently reported one profile of Kuder mean scores on the 10 scales. Motto calculated two similar Kuder mean profiles: one for subjects who completed the vocational training program and were successfully placed in jobs, and one for those who failed to complete the program. Both researchers lost information about each subject's unique interest profile using this averaging approach. If the subjects under study resembled the norm group, the average of their scores on each scale should have been expected to fall within fairly close range of the average reported for the appropriate norm group.

Subjects of the present study did not exhibit a constricted range of interests. By comparing subjects profiles to the norms presented for boys in grades 9-12 on the *Kuder E Profile Leaflet* (1963), the researcher was able to determine the number and percentage of subjects whose Kuder scores fell at or below the 25th percentile and at or above the 75th percentile on each of the 10 scales. These results are reported in Table 21-1.

By statistical definition, the 25th and 75th percentile points include the middle 50% of a distribution. In addition, the percentage of cases falling below and above the first and third quartiles, respectively, equals 50% by design of the norm tables. This researcher found that a total of 50.2% of the scores of subjects in this study met or exceeded these "critical" points. The profiles of this group were not flat; their scores in

ATTITUDES, VALUES AND INTEREST STUDIES | 163

TABLE 21-1

Number and Percentage of 722 Subjects Whose Kuder E Scores Fell at or Beyond the 25th and 75th Percentiles[a]

Kuder Scale	Boys Scoring at or Below the 25th Percentile N	%	Boys Scoring at or Above the 75th Percentile N	%	Boys Scoring at or Beyond the Highest and Lowest Quartiles N	%
Outdoor	302	41.8	99	13.7	401	55.5
Mechanical	69	9.6	268	37.1	337	46.7
Computational	228	31.6	151	20.9	379	52.5
Scientific	264	36.6	60	8.3	324	44.9
Persuasive	131	18.1	180	24.9	311	43.0
Artistic	76	10.5	196	27.1	272	37.6
Literary	422	58.4	128	17.7	550	76.1
Musical	147	20.4	183	25.3	330	45.7
Social Service	142	19.7	247	34.2	389	53.9
Clerical	140	19.4	194	26.9	334	46.3
Total	1921	26.6	1706	23.6	3627	50.2

[a]The 25th and 75th percentile points for each interest scale were given by the Norms for Boys in Grades 9-12 presented in the Kuder E Profile Leaflet.

fact resembled the distribution in the norm group quite closely. On the basis of these results, the researcher concluded that the Kuder survey was able to reveal characteristic likes and dislikes of subjects in the 10 broad interest areas measured by the instrument.

Differences in Profiles among Trades and Grades

The second phase of this study involved determining whether or not Kuder profiles were useful for distinguishing among groups of subjects classified according to the trades for which they had elected to train in school. In this part of the study, the researcher used Kuder scores of those 565 subjects enrolled at one of the two high schools constituting the total sample for the study. The scores of those 157 students who attended the second school were withheld from the analysis. This would have enabled the researcher to replicate the finding of any significant group differences in Kuder profiles for subjects from the first school on subjects from the second school.

Kuder scores served as dependent variables in the analysis, while trade group membership served as an independent variable. Since grade level was also considered as a possible source accounting for differences in Kuder scores, it was included as a second independent variable. Thus, the researcher used a two-way 7(trade groups) X 4(grades in high school) multivariate analysis of variance treating the 10 Kuder scales simultaneously as dependent variables to test the following null hypotheses:

H_{o1}: No significant differences in Kuder profiles exist among trade groups.

H_{o2}: No significant differences in Kuder profiles exist among grade levels.

H_{o3}: No significant interaction effects exist between trade groups and grade levels.

The analysis was carried out using Finn's (1967) *FORTRAN IV Multivariance Program*. Results are reported in Table 21-2. The F ratio of 1.17 for the first main effect of trade group membership failed to reach significance at the .05 level. The researcher was unable to reject the first null hypothesis and concluded that Kuder scores were not capable of making significant discriminations among trade groups.

TABLE 21-2

Results of Multivariate Analysis of Variance Treating Kuder Scales as Dependent Variables

Effect	Degrees of Freedom ndf_1	ndf_2	F Ratio	F
Trade Groups	60	2771	1.17	N.S.
Grade Levels	30	1550	1.65	.02
Interaction	180	4664	1.02	N.S.

The F ratio of 1.65 reported in Table 21-2 for the second main effect of grade level was significant beyond the .05 probability level ($p < .02$). The researcher rejected the second null hypothesis and concluded that significant differences in Kuder profiles do exist among grade levels. This result suggests that interest patterns of trade school subjects have not crystallized. The profiles differ according to grade level.

Finally, the F ratio of 1.02 for interaction effects was not statistically significant. While there were differences in Kuder scores among grade levels, they were the same kinds of differences over the seven trade groups.

DISCUSSION

Results of the first phase of this study contradicted the claims of Samuelson (1958) and Motto (1959) that Kuder profiles of vocational students are "flat," i.e., characterized by an absence of scores falling at or beyond the highest and lowest quartiles. Half of the scores for subjects of the present study met or exceeded these critical interpretation points which indicate the particular likes and dislikes of individuals as suggested by the Kuder *Manual* (1964).

Findings of the second phase of this study were in sharp contrast with the findings of previous researchers who conducted similar multivariate studies on the interest patterns of college preparatory students (Madaus and O'Hara, 1967; Mierzwa, 1961; and Mooney, 1969). One probable explanation for this contrast was that these previous researchers were able to classify similar job preferences of their college-bound subjects into broad clusters. Among these families of occupations, fairly firm discriminations were possible in terms of the nature of the work and the type and level of education required by each occupational cluster. On the other hand, this study of the interest dimension as a predictor of actual trade choice of vocational boys required the use of the specific trades in which subjects were in fact enrolled as criterion variables. However, as shown by the results of this study, differences among similar skilled trades, most of which were mechanically oriented, were not statistically significant.

No multivariate research prior to this study has been focused on the career choice of vocational high school students. "Noncollege" and "nonprofessional" groupings have been used by previous researchers to subsume skilled and semiskilled trades, clerical and secretarial career choices, and other job preferences requiring less stringent academic preparation than the professions (Astin, 1967; Madaus & O'Hara, 1967). In these studies, interests were found to be predictive of a general nonprofessional career group for noncollege bound students. However, the results of the present study suggest that more specific discriminations within the general skilled trades area are not possible on the basis of Kuder profiles.

Interests proved to be the best discriminator among college preparatory students with different career plans. However, it may be that the interest dimension has no relevance as a determinant of specific career choice of trade school boys beyond a general interest in mechanical activities. The importance of interest factors may be superseded by such factors as aptitudes, work values, and home background, particularly the occupation of the father. Matching interests to occupational activities for an individual is thought to be one means of fostering success, perseverance, and satisfaction in his job. It may be that the less academically oriented person is less concerned with the satisfaction offered him by his job, and much more concerned with the money it pays.

Future research should investigate the relevance of these dimensions for career choice of vocational students. Study of a variety of antecedent and concurrent cognitive, affective, and environmental factors which produce crystallization and stability of vocational choice of successful adult tradesmen would seem to be the best place to start further research. What characteristics differentiate these men from other skilled craftsmen who do not persevere in their trades? How can these successful tradesmen be distinguished from unskilled workers who did not develop easily marketable, manual skills? Answers to important questions like these require costly longitudinal research. However, the great demand for skilled craftsmen in our society, coupled with the dirth of our present knowledge about this population of workers, call for and justify the aid of federal funds which would make such intensive research possible. Cooley's (1963) overlapping longitudinal design enabled investigation of many years of the developmental process in an relatively short period of time. Application of this design for the study of skilled workers would enable researchers to find the determinants of occupational preference which are most important at various choice points in the lives of these workers.

References

Astin, H. S. Patterns of career choice over time. *Personnel and Guidance Journal,* 1967, *46,* 541-546.

Brayfield, A. H. The interrelation of measures of ability, aptitude, interests, and job satisfaction among clerical employees. Unpublished doctoral dissertation, University of Minnesota, 1946.

Cooley, W. W. Career development of scientists; an overlapping longitudinal study. Cooperative Research Project 436. Cambridge, Mass.: Graduate School of Education, Harvard University, 1963.

DiMichael, S. G., and Dabelstein, D. H. Work satisfaction and work efficiency of vocational rehabilitation counselors as related to measured interests (abstract), *American Psychologist,* 1947, *2,* 342-343.

Finn, J. D. *Multivariance: FORTRAN program for univariate and multivariate analysis of variance and covariance.* Buffalo: School of Education, State University of New York at Buffalo, 1967.

Hahn, M. E., and Williams, C. T. The measured interests of Marine Corps Women Reservists, *Journal of Applied Psychology,* 1945, *29,* 198-211.

Jacobs, R., and Traxler, A. E. Use of the Kuder in counseling with regard to accounting as a career, *Journal of Counseling Psychology,* 1945, *1,* 153-158.

Kuder, C. F. *Kuder E General Interest Survey.* Chicago: Science Research Associates, 1963.

Kuder, C. F. *Kuder E General Interest Survey manual.* Chicago: Science Research Associates, 1964.

ATTITUDES, VALUES AND INTEREST STUDIES | 167

Kuder, C. F. *Kuder E General Interest Survey profile leaflet*. Chicago: Science Research Associates, 1963.
Kuder, C. F. *Kuder Preference Record—Vocational, Form C*. Chicago: Science Research Associates, 1959.
Madaus, G. F., and O'Hara, R. P. Vocational interest patterns of high school boys: a multivariate approach. *Journal of Counseling Psychology*, 1967, 14, 106-112.
McRae, G. G. The relationships of job satisfaction and earlier measured interests. Unpublished doctoral dissertation, University of Florida, 1959.
Mierzwa, J. A. The differentiation of career choices: a study of a career in science during a two-year period in late adolescence. Interim Report number four of the Scientific Careers Study, Cambridge, Mass.: Graduate School of Education, Harvard University, 1961.
Mooney, R. F. Categorizing high school girls into occupational preference groups on the basis of discriminant-function analysis of interests. *Measurement and Evaluation in Guidance*, 1969, 2, 178-190.
Motto, J. J. Interest scores in predicting success in vocational school programs. *Personnel and Guidance Journal*, 1959, 37, 647-676.
North, R. D. Tests for the accounting professional. *Educational and Psychological Measurement*, 1958, 18, 691-713.
Otis-Lennon Mental Ability Test. New York: Harcourt, Brace & World, Inc., 1967.
Samuelson, C. O. Interest scores in predicting success of trade school students. *Personnel and Guidance Journal*, 1958, 36, 538-541.

Questions on the Shann article.
1. The author has claimed that the statistical techniques used in both the Samuelson and the Motto studies were inappropriate. Why were these techniques inappropriate?
2. If the author had chosen a univariate analysis of variance model for testing her null hypotheses, indicate how the wording of her null hypotheses would have to be changed.
3. The author, in testing null hypothesis 3, found no significant interaction effect. Assume for the moment that she did find a significant interaction effect. How would you interpret such an effect?
4. In general, what is the difference between a dependent and an independent variable? What is a criterion variable? What were the criterion variables of the Shann study?
5. In Table 21-2 how were the three ndf_1's arrived at?
6. In what ways does the sample used in this study limit the generalizeability of the results?

SECTION V

CONVERGENT AND DIVERGENT THINKING

22

THE DEVELOPMENT OF LOGICAL THINKING IN CHILDREN*

THOMAS C. O'BRIEN and BERNARD J. SHAPIRO
Boston University
Boston, Massachusetts

One of the goals of education, if not the goal, is the building of the child's cognitive structure (Ausubel, 1965). The height of cognitive structure according to Piaget (Inhelder and Piaget, 1958) is hypothetical-deductive thought, whereby the child is liberated from (1) his own perception of the real world and (2) the actual real world which surrounds him in order that he may then deal with (3) the concept of many possible worlds.

Suppes (1964, 1965) writes of a study performed by Hill (1960) which provided evidence, "contrary to that given by Piaget and Inhelder," that children of age six, seven, and eight "are able to deal very effectively with verbal premises that call for hypothetical reasoning and are by no means limited to 'concrete' operations." (Suppes and Binford, 1965). If this were so, it would have profound implications for one's theory of cognitive development, not to mention one's approach to educational policies.

THE HILL STUDY

In order to measure logical ability in children, Hill constructed a 100-item test involving three broad categories in elementary logic: sentential logic, classical syllogism, and logic of quantification. The test included questions such as the following:

Sentential Logic:
    If this is Room 9, then it is fourth grade.
    This is Room 9.
    Is it fourth grade?
        a. Yes   b. No

*O'Brien, Thomas C. and Shapiro, Bernard J., "The Development of Logical Thinking in Children": AMERICAN EDUCATIONAL RESEARCH JOURNAL, November 1968, pp. 531-542. Copyright by American Educational Research Association, Washington, D.C.

Classical Syllogism:
   All of Ted's pets have four legs.
   No birds have four legs.
   Does Ted have a bird for a pet?
      a. Yes   b. No

Logic of Quantifications:
   None of the pictures was painted by anyone I know.
   I know Hank's sister.
   Did she paint one of the pictures?
      a. Yes   b. No

Similarly, all items consisted of two premises, a question, and two possible responses, Yes and No. In all items the question required the student to discriminate between a necessary conclusion and the negation of a necessary conclusion.

The primary focus of the Hill study was to investigate the relationship between logical ability and age in children of age six, seven, and eight.[1] Among the findings were:

1. In the oral administration of the tests, mean scores of 71.18, 79.54, and 85.58, much higher than the 50.00 chance score were obtained by the six, seven, and eight-year-old students respectively. The mean scores in all logic categories increased with age; indeed, all differences between age-level means were statistically significant beyond the .001 level.
2. Eight-year-old students to whom the logic test had been administered in written form obtained a mean score of 86.70, not significantly different from that obtained by a comparable group of eight-year-olds to whom the test had been administered orally.
3. No statistically significant differences were detected between the mean scores of girls and those of boys.

THE PRESENT STUDY

In considering the Hill study, it was felt that the behavioral manifestation of hypothetical-deductive thinking chosen by Hill was but one of several possible behaviors. The problem was that in each of the test items a necessary conclusion followed from the premises and the task of the student in each case was simply to discern whether the third statement given was the conclusion or the negation of the conclusion. In no case was the student called upon to *test* the logical necessity of the conclusion, a behavior which the present investigators felt was vital

[1] It should be noted that other relationships were investigated in the original research which were not pursued in the present study. Among these were the effect of reinforcement on logical abilities and the relative effects of visual and oral test presentation.

to an adequate consideration of hypothetical-deductive reasoning. Therefore, the present study was undertaken to investigate the second behavior and to determine the differences, if any, between the ability of young children to discriminate between a logically necessary conclusion and its negation and their ability to test the logical necessity of a conclusion.

Two measuring instruments were used. Test A was the test used in the Hill study. Test B was the same as Test A save that (1) 33 of the original 100 items were "opened up" so that no necessary conclusion followed from the premises, and (2) for every item in Test B, a "Not Enough Clues" option was added to the "Yes" and "No" response choices provided in Test A. "Opened up" Test B items might be:

Sentential Logic:
If this is Room 9, then it is fourth grade.
This is not Room 9.
Is it fourth grade?
    a. Yes   b. No   c. Not enough clues

Classical Syllogism:
Some of Ted's pets have four legs.
No birds have four legs.
Does Ted have a bird for a pet?
    a. Yes   b. No   c. Not enough clues

Logic of Quantification:
Some of the pictures were painted by people I know.
I know Hank's sister.
Did she paint one of the pictures?
    a. Yes   b. No   c. Not enough clues

In the construction of the original test, care was taken that the content of the items be familiar but not suggestive to the students and that the vocabulary be appropriate for first, second, and third graders. These factors were also considered in the revisions necessary for the construction of Test B. In the original test (Test A), fifty items were keyed "Yes" and fifty "No." In Test B, 34, 33, and 33 items were keyed "Yes", "No" and "Not enough clues" respectively.

This study was carried out in first, second, and third grade classes in two Roman Catholic schools in upper middle class suburbs in the diocese of Cleveland, Ohio. A general description of the sample is given in Table 22-1.

Twenty-five students—12 boys and 13 girls—were randomly assigned to each of the two tests at each age-grade level. Tests were administered orally to individual first and second graders and in written

TABLE 22-1

The Sample

	Grade 1 Age 6	Grade 2 Age 7	Grade 3 Age 8
Boys	24	24	24
Girls	26	26	26
Total	50	50	50
Mean IQ[a]	110.16	111.90	116.94

[a]As measured by the Kuhlmann-Anderson Intelligence Tests, Seventh Edition.

form to the third grade group. As in the Hill study, the following precautions were taken:

1. Each student received a different randomization of test items with the restrictions that no more than three identical answers or two like principles of logic appeared consecutively.
2. Prior to the testing, time was taken with each subject to explain the general procedure and ensure that he or she understood the instructions.
3. In order to avoid undue fatigue, the tests were administered in two sessions, the 60 items from sentential logic being given in the first administration and the 40 items from the classical syllogism and the logic of quantification categories in the second.

ANALYSIS OF DATA

The data were submitted to two major analyses. The first was an analysis of the effect of age and sex factors on children's performance, each of the tests being considered separately. The second was a gradewise comparison of the children's performance on Test A with that on Test B. In each case analysis of covariance was used with IQ as the covariate. Each analysis was done for each of the three broad logic categories in the test—(1) sentential logic (60 items), (2) classical syllogism (13 items), and (3) logic of quantification (27 items)—as well as for (4) the total test (100 items), (5) the unaltered items (67 items), and (6) the altered items (33 items).

RESULTS

The analysis of Test A results confirmed much of Hill's original findings. The scores were roughly at the same high level as those reported by Hill and later confirmed, for second grade students, by Osborne (1966). As with the Hill study, there were no statistically significant differences due to sex and no statistically significant age x sex interactions. Additionally, as in the Hill study, there were significant differences ($\alpha = .01$) between age level means. Unlike the Hill research, however, where all differences between age level means were found to be statistically significant (by use of multiple t tests), Scheffe's 'a posteriori' tests for the present data showed statistically significant differences only between the means of the six-year-olds and those of the seven and eight-year-olds. As can be seen in Table 22-2 which presents the adjusted Test A means and F-ratios for the analyses of covariance, little growth was detected between age 7 and age 8, and in some cases, an actual decline took place.

TABLE 22-2

Test A Adjusted Means
(Unadjusted Means in Parentheses)

	Age 6	Age 7	Age 8	F 2,71
Sentential Logic	45.44	49.83	48.85	5.74**
(60 items)	(45.20)	(49.52)	(49.40)	
Classical Syll.	8.80	11.42	11.57	23.06**
(13 items)	(8.72)	(11.32)	(11.76)	
Logic of Quantif.	19.57	23.05	25.51	9.20**
(27 items)	(19.40)	(22.84)	(22.88)	
Total Test	73.81	83.93	82.78	13.71**
(100 items)	(73.32)	(83.32)	(83.88)	
33 Items Altered	23.44	27.26	26.78	11.77**
In Test B	(23.24)	(27.00)	(27.24)	
67 Unaltered Items	50.36	56.68	56.00	11.57**
	(50.08)	(56.32)	(56.64)	
Mean IQ	111.08	110.64	116.56	

**Significant at the one percent level.

The analyses of the Test B data produced a somewhat different picture. Again, there were no statistically significant sex differences or age x sex interactions, but unlike the Test A results, there were, with one exception, no statistically significant differences between age level means. The exception was the case of the 33 altered items. The Test B means and F-ratios are given in Table 22-3.

The second aspect of this investigation was concerned with the differences between the children's performance on the two tests at each grade level. For increased comparability of test results—Test A

176 | CONVERGENT AND DIVERGENT THINKING

TABLE 22-3
Test B Adjusted Means
(Unadjusted Means in Parentheses)

	Age 6	Age 7	Age 8	F 2,71
Sentential Logic	30.96	31.85	29.15	.59
(60 items—20 open)	(30.32)	(31.84)	(29.80)	
Classical Syll.	6.89	7.40	8.23	3.09
(13 items—4 open)	(6.64)	(7.40)	(8.48)	
Logic of Quantif.	13.09	15.41	15.54	3.15
(27 items—9 open)	(13.36)	(15.40)	(16.00)	
Total Test	51.52	54.98	54.33	1.64
(100 items—33 open)	(50.32)	(54.96)	(55.56)	
33 Altered Items	6.09	7.09	9.74	3.67*
	(5.84)	(7.08)	(10.00)	
67 Unaltered Items	45.01	47.94	44.57	1.64
	(44.08)	(47.92)	(45.52)	
Mean IQ	109.24	113.16	117.32	

*Significant at the five percent level.

items had two options and Test B items had three—student scores for this analysis were adjusted according to the standard correction formula; $S = R-(W/(n-1))$. Since sex differences had been shown to be non-significant in the previous analyses, only the test factor was investigated here. One-way analyses of covariance showed that in every case but two, the Test B mean was significantly ($\alpha = .01$) lower than the Test A mean. The Test A and Test B means and F-ratios for ages six, seven, and eight are given in Tables 22-4, 22-5, and 22-6 respectively. The two exceptions to the general trend in which Test B scores were significantly lower than Test A scores occurred at age 6 in the classical syllogisms and among the 67 unaltered items. By ages 7 and 8, however, Test A scores had risen and Test B scores had remained relatively constant so that in every case, Test B scores were significantly and substantially lower than those for Test A.

DISCUSSION

In considering the meaning of these results, it would seem that as Hill suggested, children of ages six, seven, and eight have considerable success in recognizing logically necessary conclusions. They "peak out" high and early in this ability. Children of the same age, however, experience great difficulty in testing the logical necessity of a conclusion, and

TABLE 22-4
Age 6 Adjusted Means[a]
(Unadjusted Means in Parentheses)

	Test A	Test B	F 1,47
Sentential Logic	30.18	16.02	31.86**
(60 items—20 open in Test B)	(30.40)	(15.80)	
Classical Syllogism	4.36	3.80	.38
(13 items—4 open in Test B)	(4.44)	(3.72)	
Logic of Quantification	11.68	6.92	10.69**
(27 items—9 open in Test B)	(11.80)	(6.80)	
Total Test	46.22	26.18	31.87**
(100 items—30 open in Test B)	(44.64)	(29.76)	
33 Altered Items	11.33	-7.41	122.57**
	(11.48)	(-7.56)	
67 Unaltered Items	32.89	33.15	.01
	(33.16)	(32.88)	
Mean IQ	111.08	109.24	

[a]All means are in terms of corrected scores.
**Significant at the one percent level.

TABLE 22-5
Age 7 Adjusted Means[a]
(Unadjusted Means in Parentheses)

	Test A	Test B	F 1,47
Sentential Logic	39.28	17.68	116.04**
(60 items—20 open in Test B)	(39.04)	(17.92)	
Classical Syllogism	9.73	4.83	49.94**
(13 items—4 open in Test B)	(9.64)	(4.92)	
Logic of Quantification	18.87	9.65	49.29**
(27 items—9 open in Test B)	(18.68)	(9.84)	
Total Test	67.15	32.21	134.36**
(100 items—30 open in Test B)	(66.64)	(32.72)	
33 Altered Items	21.19	-5.83	239.91**
	(21.00)	(-5.64)	
67 Unaltered Items	45.97	38.31	9.05**
	(45.64)	(38.64)	
Mean IQ	110.64	113.16	

[a]All means are in terms of corrected scores.
**Significant at the one percent level.

TABLE 22-6
Age 8 Adjusted Means
(Unadjusted Means in Parentheses)

	Test A	Test B	F 1,47
Sentential Logic	38.95	16.73	86.75**
(60 items—20 open in Test B)	(38.80)	(16.84)	
Classical Syllogism	10.57	6.43	19.61**
(13 items—4 open in Test B)	(10.52)	(6.48)	
Logic of Quantification	18.86	10.66	25.82**
(27 items—9 open in Test B)	(18.76)	(10.76)	
Total Test	68.01	33.43	63.81**
(100 items—33 open in Test B)	(67.76)	(33.68)	
33 Altered Items	21.55	-1.39	127.37**
	(21.48)	(-1.32)	
67 Unaltered Items	46.46	34.94	10.75**
	(46.28)	(35.12)	
Mean IQ	116.56	117.32	

[a]All means are in terms of corrected scores.
**Significant at the one percent level.

they show slow growth in this ability. That these two behavioral manifestations of hypothetical-deductive thinking occur at such different levels among children of the same age seems to bring into question the challenge that the original research gave to Piaget's theory regarding the growth of this kind of logical thinking in children.

One of the peculiar findings of the present research was that the children's performance on the 33 'open' items in Test B was, as is indicated by the negative corrected scores for these Test B items, below the chance level. That is, the children could have done better on these items by simple random guessing. It seems clear that for one reason or another, the children avoided the "not enough clues" response, thus indicating an avoidance of "open" situations. What the reasons for this behavior might be is at present unknown to the investigators. What is known is that the existing primary school curriculum seems to have had little effect (at least immediately) on children's tolerance of or ability to recognize "open" situations.

More than any other single thing, the present findings imply that caution should be used in the interpretation and application of the Hill research. That children of ages six, seven, and eight "are able to deal very effectively with verbal premises that call for hypothetical reasoning..." seems to suggest that there is little room for improvement in this ability in children. The data from the present study suggest, however, that hypothetical-deducive ability cannot at all be taken for granted in children of this age.

It is, of course, true that these findings must be interpreted in terms of the child's life experience. By no means do they indicate what children are *capable* of, for no attempt was made to change the subjects' hypothetical-deductive abilities. Rather, the findings refer to the current status of such thought operations in children as they result from their current life experiences. Whether such ability can be induced by some systematic influence is an open question.

Finally, it should be pointed out that this study raises many more questions than it answers. For example,
1. Children at ages six, seven, and eight scored below the chance level on the 33 "open" items in Test B. In what way does the children's ability to test for logical necessity develop at later ages? At what age does it begin to "peak out?"
2. The present samples were drawn from a population of relatively high socio-economic background. Would the same pattern of performance result with children from less fortunate backgrounds?
3. What is the relationship between a child's performance on a paper-and-pencil logic test and his performance of logical operations in everyday life situations? Further, in the light of current interest in children's ability to deal with symbolic logic (Suppes and Binford, 1965; Allen 1965), what is the relationship between children's ability in this regard and the two logical abilities previously mentioned?
4. Finally, and perhaps most importantly since this study was essentially a task of "meter-reading," what systematic influences, if any can be brought to bear to increase children's ability to test for logical necessity and to derive conclusions in hypothetical situations?

References

Allen, Layman E. "Toward Autotelic Learning of Mathematical Logic by the Wff'n Proof Games." *Monographs of the Society for Research in Child Development* 30:29-41; 1965.

Ausubel, David P. *Introduction to Readiness in the Psychology of Cognition.* New York: Holt, Rinehart and Winston, 1965. p. 9.

Hill, Shirley A. *A Study of Logical Abilities of Children.* Unpublished doctoral dissertation, Stanford University, 1960.

Inhelder, B. & Piaget, J. *The Growth of Logical Thinking From Childhood to Adolescence.* New York: Basic Books, 1958. pp. 254-255.

Osborne, Alan R. *The Effect of Two Instructional Approaches on the Understanding of Subtraction by Grade Two Pupils.* Unpublished doctoral dissertation, University of Michigan, 1966, pp. 31-39.

Suppes, Patrick. "The Ability of Elementary School Children to Learn the NEW Mathematics." *Theory Into Practice* 3:57-61; 1964.

Suppes, Patrick. "On the Behavioral Foundations of Mathematical Concepts." *Monographs of the Society for Research in Child Development* 30:90-93; 1965.

Suppes, Patrick, & Binford, Frederick. "Experimental Teaching of Mathematical Logic in the Elementary School." *The Arithmetic Teacher* 12:187-195; March 1965.

(Received January, 1968)
(Revised May, 1968)

Authors

O'Brien, Thomas C. *Address:* School of Education, Boston University, Boston, Mass. 02215 *Title:* Asst. Professor of Education *Age:* 30 *Degrees:* B.S., Iona College; M.A., Teachers College, Columbia University; Ph.D., New York University *Specialization:* Mathematics education.

Shapiro, Bernard J. *Address:* School of Education, Boston University, Boston, Mass. 02215 *Title:* Asst. Professor of Education *Age:* 33 *Degrees:* B.A., McGill University; M.A., Ed.D., Harvard University *Specialization:* Measurement, Curriculum evaluation.

Questions on the O'Brien and Shapiro article.

1. To what population can the results of this study be generalized?
2. Why did the authors use IQ as the covariate in their analyses? Random sampling is a better technique than using covariates. Why didn't the authors make use of random sampling?
3. By carefully inspecting Table 22-2 could you determine, without looking at the last row, which age level had the highest mean IQ? What is your rationale for such a determination?
4. The authors chose a one way analysis of covariance for their second analysis rather than a two way analysis. What was their justification for not using a two way analysis? Would there be any chance of obtaining sex differences if they had chosen to use a two way analysis of covariance?
5. Do you feel that the fact that the children obtained scores below what would be expected by random guessing indicates that the "open items" portion of Test B is not a valid test? Explain.
6. What other variables could have been used as covariates in this study that might have changed some of the results?

23

TEACHING CRITICAL THINKING IN ELEMENTARY SOCIAL STUDIES*

FRANCIS P. HUNKINS
University of Washington
Seattle, Washington

and

PHYLLIS SHAPIRO
John Carroll University
Cleveland, Ohio

A major goal of present education is the development of critical thinking abilities in pupils. These abilities can enable children to keep pace with the scientific and technological changes of modern society. The elementary school can and must play a vital role in this preparation. To be effective in this, the curriculum must consist of meaningful, purposeful experiences (1).

Critical thinking requires a stating of the exact nature of the problem to be solved. It requires the making of suggestions of what might be done. It demands that the pupil gather information which these various suggestions have indicated is needed. The pupil then must check the original suggestions against the facts which have been gathered, leaving room for the possible inclusion of new suggestions. The final requirement is the testing of the suggestions by actual or imaginative action (2).

Isidore Starr (3) has suggested that critical thinking can be employed in the social studies when dealing with historical accuracy of events, when controversial issues are being discussed, when various aspects of government, economics, and geographic areas are being considered. Obviously, the opportunities for stimulating critical thinking in the social studies are numerous. A major problem is the effectiveness of any proposed classroom procedure.

One of the most encouraging proposals to foster critical thinking is the "case method." This procedure presents a situation or a series of situations designed to stimulate in children a formulation of a principle or principles for action—to think critically. The children are required

*Reprinted from the September-October, 1967, issue of *Education*. Copyright, 1967, by The Bobbs-Merrill Company, Inc., Indianapolis, Indiana.

to give their reasons for their conclusions based on evidence of data. This requirement forces them to think in a critical manner regarding the problem or problems which the case contains. The actual use of this method to stimulate critical thinking at the elementary level is sparse. A study by Oliver and Baker (4) involved children in the seventh grade.

The present study investigated whether the case method approach was a superior way of teaching fifth-grade social studies as compared to the traditional lecture-textbook method with regard to critical thinking.

PROCEDURE: SUBJECTS

Fifty-four children in two fifth-grade classes were involved in the experiment. Both classes were composed of twenty-seven pupils. One of the classes was selected to receive the experimental instruction; the other class continued the regular textbook-lecture-centered pattern. These classes, in the same elementary school, drew their pupils from a relatively newly developed neighborhood. Most of the families were engaged in skilled and professional work making the area slightly above average when compared to other neighborhoods in the city, a 28,000 population community near Boston, Massachusetts.

In general background and achievement, the two class groups were similar. The mean IQ[1] of the experimental group was 107.63 (SD=12.93) as compared to 108.00 (SD=12.63) for the control group. The mean reading ability for the experimental group was 5.2 (SD= .9) compared with 5.2 (SD=1.3) for the control group.

EXPERIMENTAL TREATMENT

The experimental treatment covered sixteen class days. One of the investigators taught both groups guided by five major lesson plans. Ten one-page cases were written and employed with the experimental class during the course of this study. The cases dealt with various social studies areas: economics, cases one through four; equality and citizenship, cases five and six; freedoms of speech, worship, and privacy, cases seven through ten.

The children in the experimental group were given approximately thirty minutes to read each case and answer the questions listed at the end of the case. After the children had finished their work, discussion of the responses to the questions was held to afford an opportunity for the pupils to analyze the reasoning behind their answers. Since all children had the opportunity of responding in written form to the

1. The intelligence test and reading ability results were obtained from school records. The Otis Quick Scoring Test and the Stanford Achievement Test, Form N, were the tests employed.

questions prior to discussion, everyone had something to contribute. A situation was created in which verbal interaction existed not only between individual and teacher but also among the children. The discussion period can be considered the point at which the children received active practice in developing critical thinking skills.

To afford the reader a better idea as to the nature of the cases and questions, a sample case is included.

AN INTERESTING CONVERSATION

In this period of time "coffee shops" were very popular places where people met to discuss the news and events of the day. A Mr. Johns has just entered one and sat down and ordered a cup of coffee. While waiting to be served, a friend of his, Mr. Simes, comes over to the table and joins him. They begin a conversation concerned with the just-signed Declaration of Independence.

"What do you think of it?" asked Mr. Simes.

"Well, I think that it has a lot of new ideas, but I don't agree with all of them. The one which I do not seem to accept the most is the one which states that governments get their powers to rule from the consent of the governed. For thousands of years the rules have been set down by rulers, not the people. Look at all the progress the world has made with this type of government. Naturally, I think that some men should have authority to keep a check on the king, but as for the entire population, I'm afraid I cannot go along with that. What do they know about the problems of running a country?"

"I'm sorry, but I can't agree with you," replied Mr. Simes. "Who should have a better right to say what the government shall do than those who are to be ruled by the government?"

"But," broke in Mr. Johns, "most of the people if given the chance to make judgments concerning government, would make poor judgments and so the government would fall."

"You do not have enough faith in man to adapt to the situation," stated Mr. Simes. "Man if given the chance to rule himself can do a most effective job. Just because it has never been tried before does not mean that the results will be failure."

Questions:
1. If you could join Mr. Simes and Mr. Johns, what would be your opinion concerning this matter or problem?
2. Why would you answer in a certain way? With whom do you agree? Why?
3. What would happen if we followed Mr. Johns' idea? Mr. Simes? Can you state any examples which would give proof to your statements.
4. What lesson, if any, can be learned from reading this story?
5. Do you think that the men in the story are basing their reasoning on fact or feeling? Explain.
6. Have you heard or read of a situation similar to the one present in this story?
7. To what sources would you go to find additional information on this particular topic?

The discussion period forced the children to take positions and to analyze their standpoints with regard to standards which they had accepted as right. The children discovered that rightness and/or wrongness of questions or positions taken was a matter of degree and that once agreement upon a position was taken, a consistency in reasoning was required. The class saw that in order to critically interpret the cases, they had to analyze the information to see if it agreed with the norms of the particular period of time under consideration. The case discussion periods forced the children to consider the world of which they were a part. The class discovered that happenings and behaviors could be better understood when scrutinized. The pupils seemed to develop a probing attitude after experiencing these discussions.

In the teaching of the experimental group, the investigator employed the use of class discussion, oral book reports, written reports, outside reading, and supplementary texts to furnish the necessary background for analyzing the cases.

With the control group similar enrichment activities were used except for the omission of the class discussion and the specially prepared case materials.

The criterion tests administered before and after the experimental period were Forms A and B of the *Behavior Preference Record.* These tests were considered to be appropriate to measure the critical thinking abilities of the children. The tests measured how well the students could analyze a situation and the consistency of their actions in relation to their choices.

TABLE 23-1
Means, SD's, and Tests of Significance for Criterion Test Scores of Both Groups

Group	Pretest Mean	Pretest SD	Post-test Mean	Post-test SD	Test of Significance
Experimental (Case-method)	71.78	14.34	87.41	6.35	5.37*
Comparison (Lecture-textbook)	71.93	11.44	73.59	9.71	1.36

*Significant at the .001 level.

RESULTS AND DISCUSSION

Table 23-1 summarizes the criterion test scores of both groups and the t-tests of significance.

A statistically significant difference in critical thinking occurred for the "case method" group during the experimental period. The results indicated that no significant change in critical thinking occurred for pupils in the "lecture-textbook" class. The case method approach was thus demonstrated to be more effective in stimulating pupils' critical thinking abilities than the lecture-textbook method. The results clearly indicate that elementary school children can be taught to think critically, and that using the case method is effective.

From this research, one can deduce that a need for educational materials to stimulate critical thinking at the elementary school level exists. This present research suggests that there is merit in the idea of developing materials to satisfy this educational need.

Much more research is suggested by these results. Additional studies should be designed involving research employing case materials. Studies of such materials used by children from various socio-economic backgrounds should be considered. Studies using more cases covering a wider range of concept situations should be initiated. The number, variety, and sophistication of the questions accompanying the cases deserve attention in subsequent studies. Another important aspect to be considered in the future is the teacher-pupil verbal interaction which exists when the cases are used. This aspect could be considered along the lines of Bellack's and Aschner's work (5, 6).

Additionally beneficial to education would be a study using cases concerned with other areas of the curriculum such as science, reading, and geography. Tests in greater numbers are needed to measure the several dimensions of critical thinking (7).

References

1. Moffat, Maurice P., and Howell, Hazel W., *Elementary Social Studies Instruction* (New York: Longmans, Green and Co., 1952).
2. Bostwick, Prudence, "The Nature of Critical Thinking and Its Use in Problem Solving," *Twenty-Fourth Yearbook* (Washington, D.C.: National Council for the Social Studies, 1954).
3. Starr, Isidore, "The Nature of Critical Thinking and Its Application in the Social Studies," *Skill Development in the Social Studies* (Washington, D.C.: National Council for the Social Studies, 1963).
4. Oliver, Donald, and Baker, Susan, "The Case Method," *Social Education,* Vol. XXIII (January, 1959), pp. 25-28.
5. Bellach, Arno, and Davitz, Joel R., *The Language of the Classroom* (New York: Teachers College, Columbia University, 1963).
6. Aschner, Mary Jane, and Gallagher, J. J., *A System for Classifying Thought Processes in the Context of Classroom Verbal Interaction* (Champaign-Urbana, Illinois: University of Illinois, 1961).
7. Ennis, Robert H., "Needed: Research in Critical Thinking," *Educational Leadership,* Vol. XXI (October, 1963), pp. 17-20; 39.

Questions on the Hunkins and Shapiro article.
1. Are you convinced that both the experimental and control groups were equal on all important variables before the start of the experiment? If you are not, give your reasons.
2. Can you detect any internal validity violations that might have influenced the results of this research?
3. Would you consider this research to be experimental or non-experimental in nature? Why?
4. Referring to the table, why do the standard deviations drop considerably from pre tests to post tests?
5. Referring to the same table, do the differences in pre test standard deviations suggest that the two groups are not from the same population? Explain.
6. Are the computed t ratios results of t tests for correlated data or uncorrelated data? Why is it important for the researcher to choose the correct t test?

24

TEACHERS' RATINGS OF PUPIL CREATIVITY*

DONALD J. TREFFINGER
Purdue University
Lafayette, Indiana

and

RICHARD E. RIPPLE
Cornell University
Ithaca, New York

In assessing the validity of tests of creative thinking abilities, evidence for criterion-related validity has been difficult to obtain. One criterion which has been utilized is teacher nominations of pupils' creative abilities (Torrance, 1966). Teachers' ratings have been criticized severely, however, by a number of scholars. Holland (1959) concluded that teacher ratings were of limited valued as predictors of creativity. Piers, Daniels, and Quackenbush (1960) and Merrifield, Gardner, and Cox (1964) reported generally low correlations between teacher ratings and pupils' scores on selected measures of divergent production abilities.

Guilford (1967) concluded:

> Teachers' ratings of creative disposition of students can be readily questioned on logical and empirical grounds. It is very doubtful that the ordinary schoolroom offers opportunities for observing all the significant aspects of creative behavior that would provide an adequate basis for making judgments. It is doubtful that the average teacher knows just what to look for or understands fully the characteristics to be rated, even when the variables are broken down and explained (p. 164).

Teachers' ratings have also been criticized when the variable rated was a pupil personality characteristic or adjustment (e.g., Basumalik, 1959; Sarason, Davidson, Lighthall, Waite, and Ruebush, 1960; Treffinger and Ripple, 1967), or when the teachers' judgments about pupil behavior problems were compared with the judgments of clinicians (Wickman, 1928; Beilin, 1959). Teachers' nominations of gifted

---

*Reprinted by permission of authors and *Child Study Journal*, Vol. 1, No. 1, Fall 1970. The assistance of Mr. Neil Rosenblum in the preparation of this manuscript is gratefully acknowledged.

and intellectually superior pupils have also been criticized. Gallagher (1964) concluded, for example, that teachers have not appeared effective, when their nominations of gifted children were compared with IQ scores. Pegnato and Birch (1959) concluded that teachers did not locate gifted children with sufficient efficiency to place much reliance on them for screening purposes. Although many studies have suggested that teachers simply lack good judgment, Beilin (1959) argued that this allegation does not satisfactorily account for the problems in teachers' ratings. Often the teacher and the comparison criterion may provide ratings based on essentially different criteria. For example, in identifying behavior problems, when the kind of problem to be identified is not clearly specified, teachers may stress aggressive, disruptive behavior, whereas clinicians are more likely to be concerned with withdrawal behavior. Treffinger and Ripple (1967) also found a significant interaction between sex of teacher and sex of pupil as a factor influencing the accuracy of teachers' rankings of pupil anxiety.

It seems possible, thus, that when teachers are asked to rate their pupils' creative thinking abilities, low correlations may result from inadequate clarification of the construct to be rated, as well as from the basic inability of the teacher to assess such abilities. In addition, it is of interest to inquire whether the interaction between sex of teacher and sex of pupil, observed in another study for ratings of pupil anxiety (Treffinger and Ripple, 1967), will also occur in studying teachers' ratings of pupil creativity. Thus, the purposes of this study were:

(1) To investigate the relationship between teachers' rankings and pupils' test ranks for verbal creative thinking abilities, when the construct to be rated was defined for the teacher;

(2) To investigate the criterion-related validity of the Torrance Tests of Creative Thinking, Research Edition, Verbal Form A (Torrance, 1966) using the teacher ranking data as a criterion for such validity;

(3) To investigate whether there is a significant interaction between sex of teacher and sex of pupil with respect to teachers' rankings of pupil creativity;

(4) To investigate whether either sex of pupil's creativity is ranked with less discrepancy from test ranks by the teacher, or whether either sex of teacher ranks *all* pupils' creativity with less discrepancy between teacher and test ranks.

PROCEDURE

Six male and six female teachers were randomly selected from a pool of 16 classes which had participated in the Elementary School Creativity Project (Treffinger and Ripple, 1968). Pupils in each of these classes had received the Torrance Tests of Creative Thinking, Research

Edition, Verbal Form A (Torrance, 1966). The pupils' standardized total test scores were converted to ranks, within class, so that high test scores (high creativity) were denoted by a *low* numerical rank.

Each teacher was provided with a copy of the *Definition of Creative Thinking,* developed by Dacey (1966) for teacher use, and the form *Teacher Ranking of Pupil Creativity* (Treffinger, 1967). The definition of creativity provided a general description of creative thinking, as well as illustrations of specific pupil behaviors associated with creative performance. The teachers were asked to observe their pupils daily for one week, with respect to the behaviors specified; this was intended to establish a specific definition of creative thinking which was both consistent with the construct measured by the Torrance tests and generally equivalent for all teachers in the sample. None of the teachers had any knowledge of the pupils' test scores. After the one week observation period, the teachers were asked to rank the pupils in their classes on creativity. A rank of *one* indicated the highest rank, or *highest* estimate of creative ability. A numerical rank equivalent to the number of pupils in the class indicated the *lowest* estimate. For each class, Spearman rank order correlations (Guilford, 1965) were computed, comparing the teachers' ranks with the pupils' test ranks.

To investigate sex differences and the interaction of sex of teacher and sex of pupil, a two-way analysis of variance design was used (Guenther, 1964). The dependent variable was the mean difference between the teachers' ranking and the test ranks, by class, for all pupils of a given sex in each class. The ranks used in obtaining the mean rank differences were based on ranks assigned to the class as a whole; i.e., pupils were not reranked by sex.

RESULTS

Correlational data. Table 24-1 summarizes the rank order correlations between teachers' ranks and test ranks, by sex of teacher.

None of the F-ratios was significant at the .05 level. The difference between means by sex of teacher approached significance (6.18 vs. 5.01, $F = 3.105$, p less than .10). There was no significant interaction between sex of teacher and sex of pupil.

DISCUSSION

The correlational data provide evidence supporting the criterion-related validity of the Torrance tests of verbal creativity. Although there was considerable variability among teachers, particularly among male teachers, the magnitude of the correlations suggests considerable agreement between teacher ranks and test ranks for *most* teachers.

CONVERGENT AND DIVERGENT THINKING

TABLE 24-1

Teacher	N	Rho
Male #1	23	.28
Male #2	26	.37
Male #3	27	.26
Male #4	21	.61**
Male #5	22	.08
Male #6	18	.19
Female #1	22	.48*
Female #2	18	.48*
Female #3	21	.51*
Female #4	28	.51**
Female #5	24	.61**
Female #6	19	.34
Mean[1]		.405

[1] Derived using Fisher's z-transformation (Garrett, 1958).
*p .05
**p .01

TABLE 24-2

Analysis of Variance Table

Factor	SS	df	MS	F	p
Sex of Pupil	2.6800	1	2.6800	1.010	n.s.
Sex of Teacher	8.2368	1	8.2368	3.105	.10
Interaction	0.2091	1	0.2091	1	n.s.
Error	53.0623	20	2.6531		
Total	64.1882	23			

Means

Male Teachers	(all pupils)		6.18
	Male Pupils		6.43
	Female Pupils		5.94
Female Teachers	(all pupils)		5.01
	Male Pupils		5.44
	Female Pupils		4.58
	All Male Pupils		5.93
	All Female Pupils		5.26

That is, when teachers were provided with a clearly stated definition of the construct to be rated and with a specific procedure to follow, they were able to make rankings which correspond with pupils' test score rankings.

The *variability* among teachers is, however, an important consideration. What accounts for the differences among teachers? Although the answer to this question can only be a matter of speculation, several interesting possibilities exist.

The first of these is that the teachers' rankings might have been influenced by sex role differences, as suggested by previous work with anxiety ratings. There was no indication of such an interaction, however, in the analysis of variance data from this study. Also, although the discrepancy scores from the two studies are not based on rankings by the same teachers and are therefore not directly comparable, the mean discrepancies in this study are generally lower than those reported for teachers' anxiety ratings. It is possible that it may have been somewhat easier for teachers to rate pupils' verbal creativity than it had been to rate anxiety, or that more objective criteria were available to provide the basis for the ranking.

Another possibility is that either the teachers' rankings or the pupils' test scores were unreliable. This problem warrants further investigation, since no data were available concerning the reliability of the teachers' ranks. There was evidence, however, for the reliability of the Torrance test scores. Three-week test-retest reliabilities for total score, at four grade levels, ranged from .52 to .65 (Treffinger and Ripple, 1968). It should be noted that several of the observed correlation coefficients (Table 24-1) approach these limits.

It is possible that the accuracy of the teachers' rankings may have, in part, been influenced by differential utilization of the training procedures, observation period, and ranking instructions. For example, some teachers may have omitted the observation period or merely rated their pupils without giving careful consideration to the definition that was provided.

Three directions for future research are indicated: first, to investigate systematically the influences of sex differences on teachers' ratings of various pupil characteristics, by having a single sample of teachers rate several characteristics. Thus, ratings of different characteristics (e.g., personality and adjustment variables as opposed to intellectual characteristics) could be directly compared, and the differential influence of sex role factors could be examined. Secondly, there should be research to investigate the influence of specific variations in training and instructions on the accuracy of teachers' rankings and their reliability. Finally, there is a need to establish a measure of the reliability of ratings for all raters as individuals.

References

Basumallik, T. "Validity of teachers' ratings of pupils' personality traits." *Indian Journal of Psychology,* 1959, *34,* 167-177.

Beilin, H. "Teachers' and clinicians' attitude towards the behavior problems of children: a reappraisal." *Child Development,* 1959, *30,* 9-25.

Dacey, John S. "Definition of Creative Thinking Abilities." Ithaca, New York: Cornell University, Learning Structures Project, unpublished mimeo, 1966.

Gallagher, J. J. *Teaching the Gifted Child.* Boston: Allyn and Bacon, 1964.

Garrett, H. E. *Statistics in Psychology and Education.* New York: David McKay, 1958.

Guenther, W. C. *Analysis of Variance.* Englewood Cliffs, New Jersey: Prentice Hall, 1964.

Guilford, J. P. *Fundamental Statistics in Psychology and Education.* New York: McGraw-Hill, 1965.

Guilford, J. P. *The Nature of Human Intelligence.* New York: McGraw-Hill, 1967.

Holland, J. L. "Some limitations of teacher ratings as predictors of creativity." *Journal of Educational Psychology,* 1959, *50,* 219-223.

Merrifield, P. R., Gardner, S. F., and Cox, A. B. "Aptitudes and personality measures related to creativity in seventh-grade children." *Report of the Psychological Laboratory,* University of Southern California, 1964, no. 28.

Pegnato, C. V. and Birch, J. W. "Locating gifted children in junior high school: a comparison of methods." *Exceptional Children,* 1959, *25:* 300-304.

Piers, E. V., Daniels, J. M., and Quackenbush, J. F. "The identification of creativity in adolescents." *Journal of Educational Psychology,* 1950, *51,* 346-351.

Sarason, S. B., Davidson, K. S., Lighthall, F., Waite, R., and Ruebush, B. K. *Anxiety in Elementary School Children.* New York: John Wiley, 1960.

Torrance, E. P. *Torrance Tests of Creative Thinking: Norms-Technical Manual,* Princeton, New Jersey: Personnel Press, 1966.

Treffinger, D. J. "Teacher ranking of pupil creativity." Ithaca, New York: Cornell University, Elementary School Creativity Project, unpublished mimeo, 1967.

Treffinger, D. J. and Ripple, R. E. "The interaction of sex of teacher and sex of pupil as a factor affecting teachers' rankings of pupil anxiety." *Psychology in the Schools,* 1967, *4,* 331-335.

Treffinger, D. J. and Ripple, R. E. *The effects of programmed instruction in productive thinking on verbal creativity and problem solving among elementary school pupils.* Final Report of USOE Research Project OEG-0-8-080002-0220-010. Ithaca, New York: Cornell University, 1968.

Wickman, E. K. *Children's behavior and teacher's attitudes.* New York: Commonwealth Fund, 1928.

Questions on the Treffinger and Ripple article.

1. In stating the first purpose of their study the authors use the word "construct." What is a construct? How would one determine construct validity?
2. Did the number of teachers selected for this study hamper in any way the generalizeability of the authors' results? Explain.
3. Do male teachers or female teachers rank the verbal creativity of their students more similar to the rankings resulting from the Torrance test? What evidence presented in this study supports your answer?

CONVERGENT AND DIVERGENT THINKING | 193

4. In Table 24-2, what is the value of the "Within Groups" degrees of freedom?
5. Is the Spearman Rank Order Correlation used in this study as powerful a statistical technique as the Pearson Product Moment Correlation? Why?
6. List the factors which might have influenced the internal validity of this study. Recommend how each factor could have been controlled.

25

DIVERGENT THINKING DECLINES IN THE FOURTH AND SEVENTH GRADES

LISANO R. ORLANDI
Lowell State College
Lowell, Massachusetts

PURPOSE

This study was designed to investigate the validity of Torrance's hypothesis that the performance of American children in divergent thinking declines in grades 4 and 7 (Torrance, 1962, 1967). Some research exists to support Torrance's position (Axtell, 1966) but other research tends to conflict with it (Long and Henderson, 1964, and Iscoe and Pierce-Jones, 1964). Because Torrance's views have received considerable publicity, it was deemed worthwhile to examine their validity in a non-public school setting and among children from different social classes. In null form, the hypothesis of this study is as follows:

> There is no signigicant difference in the divergent thinking scores between grades 3 and 4 and between grades 6 and 7 within; (a) middle-class, (b) combined lower-class, and (c) each of four lower-class racial or ethnic groups of urban Catholic elementary school children in total fluency and total flexibility scores in separate verbal and figural measures.

DESIGN

Description of the Sample

A total of 320 children in Catholic elementary schools in grades 3, 4, 6, and 7 were studied in a cross-sectional design. Of the 320, equal groups of 64 were selected from the following five subcultural groups; Negroes, Italians, French-Canadians, and an ethnically heterogeneous middle-class group. The four homogeneous, racial and ethnic groups were all of a lower class background as determined by Hollingshead's *Two Factor Index of Social Position* (1957). The ethnically heterogeneous group was determined to be of middle-class status on the basis of the head of the household (Smith, 1965).

Each group of children came from a school in which at least 50% of the children were of the same social class status and, in the case of the four racial and ethnic groups, from a school in which at least 50% of the children were of the same racial or ethnic group.

Instruments

In order to assess the development of divergent thinking in the children, the *Torrance Tests of Creative Thinking* (1966a) were used as measures. The tests contain two separate sections—Verbal and Figural. Three of the commonly used Verbal subtests were scored for fluency and flexibility. These subtests are entitled *Ask-and-Guess, Product Improvement,* and *Unusual Uses.* Two of the commonly used Figural subtests were scored for fluency and flexibility also. The subtests are entitled *Picture Completion* and *Lines.* Thus, all subtests were scored for fluency and flexibility. The fluency score provided an index of a person's ability to produce a *large number* of ideas with either words (verbal) or by drawing figures from given stimuli, such as lines (figural). Flexibility demonstrates an individual's ability to produce a variety of *different* ideas with either words (verbal) or by drawing figures from given stimuli, such as lines (figural). In order to obtain scores on total verbal fluency, total figural flexibility, total figural fluency and total figural flexibility, the appropriate scores of verbal and figural subtests were added together as suggested in the scoring manual. Both the reliability and validity of the *Torrance Tests* are open to question. Studies of the reliability of the tests have yielded reliability coefficients as low as .34 in some cases and as high as .93 in others (Torrance, 1966). The validity of the *Torrance Tests* has been denied by Wallach (1968) who asserts that they simply test general intelligence and not a separate factor of creativity. Despite these shortcomings, the Torrance Tests are among the most widely used measures of divergent thinking and are probably the most suitable tests presently available for young children.

In order to adjust statistically for differences in intelligence, an overall measure of intelligence, the *Otis-Lennon Mental Ability Tests* (1967a), was used as a covariate. Three of the six levels of the tests were used in this study: the Elementary I Level for children in grade 3; the Elementary II Level for children in grades 4 and 6; and the Intermediate Level in grade 7. In studies of the reliability of the tests, the coefficients are quite high ranging from a low of .84 to a high of .96 in the various levels given in different grades. The Otis series of intelligence tests have been among the most respected in terms of validity. Data to support the validity of this test, which is intended to be an improvement over its precursors, is being gathered (*Otis-Lennon Mental Ability Test,* 1967b).

Statistical Analysis

In addition to the administration of the *Torrance Tests* and the *Otis-Lennon Mental Ability Tests,* each child's age in months was determined so that the differences in age in the various grade levels could be adjusted statistically. In brief, the several scores on the *Torrance*

196 | CONVERGENT AND DIVERGENT THINKING

Tests were the criterion variables in the study, and scores on the *Otis-Lennon Mental Ability Tests* and age in months served as covariates.

The analysis of the data was handled in the following manner. One-way univariate analyses of covariance were used to determine the differences between grades 3 and 4 and between grades 6 and 7 within each social class and within each ethnic and racial group in the lower class. Age in months and deviation I.Q. scores of the *Otis-Lennon Mental Ability Tests* were used as covariates in each case; total verbal fluency, total verbal flexibility, total figural flexibility were the criterion variables in each case.*

RESULTS

For both grades 3 and 4, and 6 and 7, the following procedure of presenting the data reduction and analysis will be used:
1. the adjusted means of all the groups on the criterion variables will be presented in each pair of grades;
2. a table of the tests of significance for the univariate analyses of covariance for all groups on each criterion variable will be presented along with a discussion of the results.

TABLE 25-1

Means and Standard Deviations of the Middle-Class, Combined Lower-Class, and Four Lower-Class Subcultural Groups in Grades 3 and 4 Adjusted for Intelligence and Age on Each of the Criterion Variables

Variable	Middle Class Grade 3	Middle Class Grade 4	Combined Lower Class Grade 3	Combined Lower Class Grade 4	Negro Grade 3	Negro Grade 4
Total Verbal Fluency	69.76 (15.06)	30.80	57.81 (18.66)	23.55	51.49 (19.26)	23.82
Total Verbal Flexibility	34.61 (6.45)	18.89	28.01 (7.47)	12.95	26.43 (6.39)	13.51
Total Figural Fluency	18.63 (4.35)	23.18	18.15 (6.56)	20.84	17.66 (6.97)	19.53
Total Figural Flexibility	13.99 (3.53)	18.94	13.38 (4.62)	16.59	12.17 (4.36)	15.77

*Hereafter, the following abbreviations for the scores will be used: TVFU=total verbal fluency; TVFX=total verbal flexibility; TFFU=total figural fluency; and TFFX=total figural flexibility.

TABLE 25-1—Continued

Variable	Italian Grade 3	Italian Grade 4	Irish Grade 3	Irish Grade 4	French-Canadian Grade 3	French-Canadian Grade 4
Total Verbal Fluency	68.04 (11.95)	15.02	58.24 (22.77)	20.25	58.10 (19.86)	30.46
Total Verbal Flexibility	33.05 (6.58)	9.01	27.61 (9.76)	10.83	27.32 (6.38)	15.55
Total Figural Fluency	21.50 (6.11)	19.25	19.80 (4.84)	24.02	15.12 (7.26)	19.07
Total Figural Flexibility	14.27 (5.18)	16.23	15.10 (4.05)	18.28	11.99 (4.78)	16.07

Note: The adjusted standard deviation for each variable has been inserted in parentheses below each group of adjusted means.

The null hypothesis for grades 3 and 4 was rejected in the following instances:

a. In the middle-class group on TVFU, TVFX, and TFFX because the adjusted mean score in grade 4 was significantly lower on TVFU and TVFX and significantly higher on TFFX than in grade 3;

TABLE 25-2

F Tests for Each of the Criterion Variables between Grades 3 and 4 for the Middle-class, Combined Lower-class, Combined Middle-class, and Separate Lower-class Subcultural Groups on Means Adjusted for Intelligence and Age

Variable	Middle Class F	df	Combined Lower Class F	df	Negro F	df
Total Verbal Fluency	17.745***	1, 28	52.406***	1, 124	9.966**	1, 28
Total Verbal Flexibility	15.482***	1, 28	63.179***	1, 124	19.717***	1, 28
Total Figural Fluency	2.852	1, 28	2.613	1, 124	.344	1, 28
Total Figural Flexibility	5.118*	1, 28	7.525**	1, 124	3.296	1, 28

198 | **CONVERGENT AND DIVERGENT THINKING**

TABLE 25-2—Continued

Variable	Italian		Irish		French-Canadian	
	F	df	F	df	F	df
Total Verbal Fluency	51.501***	1, 28	9.294**	1, 28	5.737*	1, 28
Total Verbal Flexibility	36.408***	1, 28	9.871**	1, 28	10.092**	1, 28
Total Figural Fluency	.352	1, 28	2.530	1, 28	.879	1, 28
Total Figural Flexibility	.373	1, 28	2.054	1, 28	2.150	1, 28

*p<.05
**p<.01
***p<.001

b. In the combined lower-class group on TVFU, TVFX, and TFFX because the adjusted mean score in grade 4 was significantly lower on TVFU and TVFX and significantly higher in TFFX than in grade 3;

c. In the four subcultural groups on TVFU and TVFX because the adjusted mean scores in grade 4 were significantly lower than in grade 3.

In brief, the significance test results between grades 3 and 4 of middle-class, combined lower-class, and four lower-class subcultural groups showed that in all groups a significant decline occurred between the grade 3 and 4 samples on TVFU and TVFX. On TFFU, no significant differences between any of the samples of any of the groups were demonstrated in grades 3 and 4. On TFFX, significant increases between the grade 3 and 4 samples in the middle-class group and the combined lower-class group were demonstrated but there were no significant differences at the .05 level in any of the four subcultural groups.

Table 25-3 contains the adjusted mean scores of each group on the criterion variables in grades 6 and 7. Table 25-4 contains the results of the univariate analyses of covariance for each group in these grades.

The null hypothesis for grades 6 and 7 was rejected in the following instances:

a. In the middle-class group, there were no significant differences between grades 6 and 7 on any of the criterion variables;

b. In the combined lower-class group, because the adjusted mean scores of the grade 7 sample were higher than the grade 6 sample on all four criterion variables;

c. (1) In the Negro sample on TVFU, TFFU, and TFFX because the adjusted mean score of these variables was higher in grade 7 than in grade 6;

(2) In the Italian sample on TVFU and TVFX because the adjusted mean score of these variables was higher in grade 7 than in grade 6;

(3) In the Irish and French-Canadian samples, there were no significant differences on any of the criterion variables between grades 6 and 7.

In brief, the significance test results of middle-class, combined lower-class, and four lower-class subcultural groups showed that there was a significant increase on all four criterion variables for the combined lower-class group, on TVFU, TFFU, and TFFX for Negro children, and on TVFU and TVFX for the Italian children. The null hypothesis was not rejected between grades 6 and 7 on all four criterion variables for the middle-class sample and for the Irish and French-Canadian samples, on TVFX for the Negro sample, and on TFFU and TFFX for the Italian sample.

TABLE 25-3

Means and Standard Deviation of the Middle-class, Combined Lower-class, and Four Lower-class Subcultural Groups in Grades 6 and 7 Adjusted for Intelligence and Age on Each of the Criterion Variables

Variable	Middle Class		Combined Lower Class		Negro	
	Grade 6	Grade 7	Grade 6	Grade 7	Grade 6	Grade 7
Total Verbal Fluency	54.53	70.03	38.81	53.56	34.63	61.37
	(28.58)		(18.04)		(17.62)	
Total Verbal Flexibility	27.44	30.69	20.07	23.62	20.27	24.85
	(9.06)		(6.74)		(6.66)	
Total Figural Fluency	21.14	17.86	21.02	24.54	17.76	23.62
	(7.85)		(6.21)		(4.37)	
Total Figural Flexibility	16.75	14.13	15.97	19.05	12.89	18.93
	(5.91)		(4.45)		(3.72)	

TABLE 25-3—Continued

Variable	Italian Grade 6	Italian Grade 7	Irish Grade 6	Irish Grade 7	French-Canadian Grade 6	French-Canadian Grade 7
Total Verbal Fluency	46.13	65.43	43.27	35.60	37.44	45.62
	(16.47)		(15.44)		(15.58)	
Total Verbal Flexibility	19.24	27.13	24.55	17.07	19.13	22.49
	(5.28)		(7.74)		(5.56)	
Total Figural Fluency	23.30	28.32	24.11	22.02	20.02	23.11
	(5.89)		(6.59)		(6.38)	
Total Figural Flexibility	17.01	21.31	18.03	17.66	16.34	17.91
	(4.60)		(4.11)		(4.68)	

Note: The adjusted standard deviation for each variable has been inserted in parentheses below each group of adjusted means.

TABLE 25-4

F Tests for Each of the Criterion Variables between Grades 6 and 7 for the Middle-Class, Combined Lower-class, and Separate Lower-class Subcultural Groups on Means Adjusted for Intelligence and Age

Variable	Middle Class F	Middle Class df	Combined Lower Class F	Combined Lower Class df	Negro F	Negro df
Total Verbal Fluency	1.016	1, 28	11.718***	1, 124	9.181**	1, 28
Total Verbal Flexibility	.444	1, 28	4.875*	1, 124	1.883	1, 28
Total Figural Fluency	.604	1, 28	5.644*	1, 124	7.158*	1, 28
Total Figural Flexibility	.681	1, 28	8.441**	1, 124	10.522**	1, 28

CONVERGENT AND DIVERGENT THINKING | 201

TABLE 25-4—Continued

Variable	Italian		Irish		French-Canadian	
	F	df	F	df	F	df
Total Verbal Fluency	4.887*	1, 28	.645	1, 28	1.647	1, 28
Total Verbal Flexibility	7.938**	1, 28	2.437	1, 28	2.185	1, 28
Total Figural Fluency	2.588	1, 28	.263	1, 28	1.401	1, 28
Total Figural Flexibility	3.110	1, 28	.021	1, 28	.677	1, 28

*$p<.05$
**$p<.01$
***$p<.001$

CONCLUSION

The tests of significance (intended to test Torrance's hypotheses of fourth-grade and seventh-grade declines in American children) among parochial school children resulted in significant declines on TVFU and TVFX for all groups of children in grade 4. This decline did not occur on TFFU and TFFX. Rather, a significant increase occurred in the adjusted mean scores of the middle-class and combined lower-class groups on TFFX. The purported seventh grade decline did not occur on any of the criterion variables. In fact, there was some evidence to indicate that an increase rather than a decrease occurred in the seventh grade in that the combined lower-class group did increase significantly on all four criterion variables. The Negro group increased on three and the Italian group on two criterion variables.

Thus, the significance test results supported Torrance's view of a decline in divergent thinking only in verbal measures in the fourth grade and not at all in the seventh grade. Even the decline in divergent thinking in verbal scores in the fourth grade is open to serious question because the difference may be attributable to other factors than grade level. For example, the difference was, it seems, at least partly attributable to the fact that verbal tests were orally administered to children in grade 3; whereas children in grade 4 were administered a group, written, verbal test, as the test manual indicated was acceptable. However, in retrospect, it appears obvious that children in grade 4, and even in higher grades, demonstrate a lack of facility in the mechanics of writing and are often more concerned with the shaping of letters than they are with the production of ideas. Thus, the restriction of the writing situation must be taken into account in interpreting any divergent test score results in verbal areas. There are still other plausible explanations for the decline in verbal divergent performance in grade 4 than those presented here, but it is enough to point out that grade level is not the only explanation for a decline.

SUMMARY

Torrance's hypothesis of a fourth-and seventh-grade decline among American children was examined through a study including 320 children in urban Catholic parochial schools from five subcultural groups —one group of middle-class children, and four groups of lower-class children of different racial and ethnic backgrounds. The results of the study generally did not concur with Torrance's hypothesis of a decline in divergent thinking performance in grade 4 and grade 7. In that part of the study in which there was a decline befitting Torrance's hypothesis, the decline, it was pointed out, could have been attributed to factors other than grade level.

References

Axtell, J. Discontinuities in the perception of curiosity of gifted adolescents. *The Gifted Child Quarterly,* 1966, 10, 78-82.

Hollingshead, A. B. Two factor index of social position. New Haven, Conn., 1957.

Iscoe, I., & Pierce-Jones, J. Intelligence in white and negro children. *Child Development,* 1964, 35, 785-797.

Long, B. H., & Henderson, E. H. Opinion formation and creativity in elementary school children. *Psychological Reports,* 1965, 17, 219-223.

Otis, A. S., & Lennon, R. T. *Otis-Lennon mental ability test.* New York: Harcourt, Brace & World, 1967. (a)

Otis, A. S., & Lennon, R. T. *Otis-Lennon mental ability test: Manual for administration.* New York: Harcourt, Brace & World, 1967. (b)

Smith, R. M. The relationship of creativity of social class. Cooperative Research Project No. 2250, July, 1965.

Torrance, E. P. Cultural discontinuities and the development of originality of thinking. *Exceptional Children,* 1962, 29, 2-13.

Torrance, E. P. *Torrance tests of creative thinking.* Princeton, N. J.: Personnel Press, 1966. (a)

Torrance, E. P. *Torrance tests of creative thinking: Norms-technical manual.* (Research Ed.) Princeton, N. J.: Personnel Press, 1966. (b)

Torrance, E. P. *Understanding the fourth grade slump in creative thinking.* Cooperative Research Project No. 994, December, 1967.

Wallach, M. A. Review of E. P. Torrance, *Torrance Tests of Creative Thinking. American Educational Research Journal,* 1968, 5, 272-280.

Wallach, M. A. & Kogan, N. *Modes of thinking in young children: A study of the creativity-intelligence distinction.* New York: Holt, Rinehart and Winston, 1965.

Questions on the Orlandi article.

1. In the section on the Purpose of the study, the author presents one null hypothesis but, in actuality, there are a number of null hypotheses contained within the one presented. How many null hypotheses are there? Explain the reason for your answer.
2. Why did the author use the statistical technique of analysis of covariance on the data rather than analysis of variance?
3. In what way do the adjusted means and adjusted standard deviations of Tables 25-1 and 25-3 differ from unadjusted means and unadjusted standard deviations?
4. In Tables 25-2 and 25-4, explain the reason for the number of degrees of freedom for each group.
5. In Tables 25-2 and 25-4, explain what is meant by (a) F tests, and (b) $p < .05$?
6. In the section on Conclusions, the author states there are "other plausible explanations for the decline in verbal divergent performance in grade 4 than those presented here." What other plausible explanations are there?